MW01147418

The Forgotten 1970
CHICAGO CUBS

The Forgotten 1970 CHICAGO CUBS

GO AND GLOW

William S. Bike

THE
History
PRESS

Published by The History Press
Charleston, SC
www.historypress.com

Copyright © 2021 by William S. Bike
All rights reserved

Front cover, top left: National Baseball Hall of Fame Library; *top center*: Chicago History Museum, ICHi-024309; F.S. Dauwalter, photographer; *top right*: Photo 112145772 © Sports Images/Dreamstime.com; *bottom*: "Mr. Cub" Ernie Banks signs autographs before a 1970 game at Wrigley Field. Banks played all of his eighteen seasons with the Cubs, was an eleven-time All-Star, the National League MVP in 1958 and 1959 and was inducted into the National Baseball Hall of Fame in 1977. David Durochik via AP.
Back cover: National Baseball Hall of Fame Library; *inset*: Chicago National League Ball Club Inc. (Chicago Cubs).

First published 2021

Manufactured in the United States

ISBN 9781467149082

Library of Congress Control Number: 2021931241

Notice: The information in this book is true and complete to the best of our knowledge. It is offered without guarantee on the part of the author or The History Press. The author and The History Press disclaim all liability in connection with the use of this book.

All rights reserved. No part of this book may be reproduced or transmitted in any form whatsoever without prior written permission from the publisher except in the case of brief quotations embodied in critical articles and reviews.

CONTENTS

PREFACE

Sure, the 1969 Chicago Cubs' year was great; any Cub fan around then will never forget it.

My favorite Cub year, however, was 1970, when I was thirteen years old. My favorite players were Billy Williams and Jim Hickman, and they had their best years. I liked the new players the Cubs had acquired before and during the season—Tommy Davis, Cleo James, J.C. Martin, Milt Pappas, Joe Pepitone and Roberto Rodriguez among them. I kept scrapbooks (invaluable source material for this book) in 1970, cutting out newspaper clippings about all of the games.

I had tickets for the Cubs' October 3 and October 4 playoff games—if only the Cubs had qualified for them. The pennant race, which throughout September saw the Pirates, Mets and Cubs separated by one game or less, was the closest Cub pennant race of my lifetime; even when they won division titles in later years, the Cubs did it somewhat easily. The 1970 Eastern Division pennant race ranks with the 1964 National League, the 1967 American League and the 1978 American League Eastern Division races in terms of pressure, excitement and surprise.

When I opened up a package of Topps baseball cards and found a Cub card in it, jubilation ensued. I truly believe I saw at least part of every Cub game broadcast on WGN-TV that year—and almost all of them were. A few of those West Coast games were not on TV because they started at 10:00 p.m., so all the other Cubs fans and I listened on a transistor radio. Even when I was in St. Sylvester's School in April, May and September, we

The Cubs were so close to winning their division in September that the National League authorized management to print playoff tickets. *Collection of William S. Bike, Chicago National League Ball Club Inc. (Chicago Cubs).*

kids could get home and catch the last few innings—unless Fergie Jenkins pitched one of his sub-two-hour gems. My dad, William F. Bike, always seemed more confident about a Cub victory when Jenkins took the mound.

Because of 1969, however, not every kid remained so devoted to the 1970 Cubs. My St. Sylvester's buddy Karl Matuszewski recalled: "After the '69 heartbreak, I lost all interest in baseball. I was so young and impressionable. I no longer listened to games on my transistor or watched on TV."[1]

Many Cub fans, experiencing the heartaches of 1969, 1984, 1989 and 2003, can relate. Back in 1970, however, many of us were ready to believe again.

The Cubs had moved Ladies' Day from Thursday to Friday in 1970, so my mom, Jean Bike, and my St. Sylvester's school buddy Mike Giannetto's mom, Angie Giannetto, took us to a lot of Friday games. The play *Bleacher Bums* had it right—back then, often the moms knew more about the Cubs than the dads did, since the Cubs played during the day when the dads worked. Many moms worked as homemakers in those days, Cub games were always on TV on WGN during the day and the moms could actually go to the games for free with us kids on Fridays.

A 1970 Chicago Cubs scorecard cost only fifteen cents and featured an artist's rendering of a Cub infielder turning a double play. *Collection of Ken Hennig, Chicago National League Ball Club Inc. (Chicago Cubs).*

Thirteen-year-old female classmates of mine that year would tell the Chicago Transit Authority bus driver that they were twelve to get the cheaper child's transit fare; then, when they got to Wrigley Field, they suddenly were fourteen so they could get in for free on Ladies' Day.

My mother's favorite player that year was Johnny Callison, because, she said at the time, he "walks like a tough guy."

I kept score for every game I attended—even both ends of doubleheaders. Hey, the scorecards cost only fifteen cents!

We were disheartened when the Cubs released veteran pitcher Ken Johnson in April. The previous year, Mike and I headed down to the front row of the lower deck box-seat area before a game to get Johnson's autograph when an usher decided to try to stop us by picking Mike up by his head! Johnson yelled at the usher to put Mike down, and the Cub made a point of signing our autographs and taking time to talk with us. Twenty years later, with Johnson working for a college, as I was, I spoke to him on the phone and was pleased that he remembered the incident.

A buddy and I attended the April 18 game in which Johnson pitched against the Cubs with me cheering him on, an extremely rare instance of my rooting for a Cub opponent.

My dad enjoyed watching the weekend and road night games on TV with my mom and me, but since he worked seven days a week as a truck driver, he had not actually been to Wrigley Field since 1937, when he sat in the old field-level bleachers that Cub management tore down during the season from July through September, replaced by the iconic ivy-covered outfield walls.

My mother, our friends and I saw some classic games at Wrigley Field that year, mostly on Fridays, but we loved the Cubs so much we would shell out a couple of dollars to occasionally go another day as well.

My grade-school buddy Roman Barczynski and I went to the May 13 game by ourselves because St. Sylvester's gave us Wednesday afternoons off. In that one, the Cubs' Ernie Banks broke up New York Met Gary Gentry's no-hitter, and Roman and I saw ourselves on TV on the replays on the news that night. My mom and I also went to a rare Saturday doubleheader on May 30 to see Ernie Banks and Billy Williams honored.

On a Friday in May in which the Cubs started a four-game series against the Mets, a kid had put a nasty word on the cork board in our homeroom at St. Sylvester's School at lunchtime. When the nun whose classroom it was came back from lunch, she saw the word and called the principal, and they demanded that we kids tell them who did it by Monday or there would be dire, dire consequences. We thought about doing so, but after the Cubs won three out of four in New York, we felt so jubilant that we decided to keep silent. Talk of punishment turned out to be a bluff, and the kid got away with it. The Cubs had saved him!

Rarely did my dad have time to take me to a game, but that happened on May 21 for the Cubs–White Sox Boys' Benefit night game at Comiskey Park, where we saw Hickman hit a home run onto the roof.

My mother and I were at Wrigley Field with Mike and Angie on June 19 for a seventeen-inning loss to St. Louis (*of course* we stayed for the full game) and for a 16–14 loss to Pittsburgh on July 3. WGN-TV broadcaster Jack Brickhouse, when relief pitchers Ted Abernathy and Hank Aguirre warmed up, would say, "Ab and Ag in the bullpen." When the Cubs foolishly traded Abernathy, Mike quipped, "Ag lost his Ab."

My mom and I went to a 7–4 win against the Mets on September 4 in the heat of the pennant race; in the huge standing-room crowd, she found a single, grandstand seat on the aisle, and sat I on the concrete step next to her, to the chagrin of all the vendors trying to climb the stairs with their wares.

My St. Sylvester's friends Irene Pasulka and the late Dave Skrzypczynski and I planned to attend the September 13 game, but Irene could not go at the last minute, and Dave did not want to go either, because of the rain. So we all stayed home and watched the game on our TVs. In that game, in the heat of the pennant race, the Pittsburgh Pirates' Matty Alou dropped a fly ball in the ninth inning, and the Cubs ended up winning the game. Had the Cubs taken the pennant, that contest would have been the turning point—except, we were not there. Now Irene is Dr. Irene O'Neill, and we still laugh about missing the game.

Another grade school buddy, John Motyka, and I bought Cub playoff tickets for the games that would have been played in Wrigley Field on October 3 and 4—a weekend, so we would not have missed any school. In that simpler time, the Cubs ran an ad in the newspapers saying tickets were on sale, and John went down to Wrigley, walked up to the ticket window and bought them. We got our money back when the Cubs did not make it.

I had no inkling at the time, but the 1970 Cubs' season would be the last one of my youth, when I still had a child's admiration for baseball players as heroes. A year later, the Cubs were still good but never really contended, I quit keeping scrapbooks and collecting baseball cards, I started going to more games with my buddies and fewer with my mother and I graduated from grade school and entered Gordon Tech High School. Fortunately, my mother and I did see Milt Pappas's 1972 no-hitter in person together.

There comes a time when we all must put away our toys and become men and women. Thankfully for me, that time had not yet come in 1970, and I could enjoy every minute of the 1970 Chicago Cubs—the best damn team never to win a pennant.

ACKNOWLEDGEMENTS

T hank you to:

everyone involved with this book, including all the newspaper and magazine writers and book authors whose works I cited, and all the photographers whose photos I included;

Gazette Chicago writer Gabija Steponenaite, who suggested I write another book;

Adam Kivel, a writer and baseball fan, who did his usual great editing job when examining the manuscript for this work;

my wife, Anne Nordhaus-Bike, for providing inspiration and encouragement, and for being a fan of center fielder Cleo James;

Rick Delaney and Ben Gibson of Arcadia Publishing/The History Press, with whom I worked closely to make the book a reality;

John Horne of the National Baseball Hall of Fame Library, Katie Levi of the Chicago History Museum and Mary Frances Trucco of Jewel-Osco, for help with photos;

the current Ricketts family ownership and management of the Chicago Cubs, who brought us a World Series title in 2016, and to the Cubs' Lacey Christopherson, whom I worked with on some photos; and

to the members of the 1970 Cubs, who brought Cub fans both joy and heartbreak during another fun Cub season.

Barney Sterling was the Chicago Cubs' photographer in the 1960s and early 1970s, so he likely shot some of the photos used with the permission of the Chicago Cubs.

Major League Baseball trademarks and copyrights are used with permission of Major League Baseball. Visit MLB.com.

Composite photo of 1970 team courtesy of the Chicago National League Ball Club Inc. (Chicago Cubs).

1

PROLOGUE

1969

Every Chicago Cubs fan, and pretty much every baseball fan, knows the story of the 1969 National League pennant race. From Opening Day against Philadelphia, when the Cubs won on an eleventh-inning Willie Smith home run, and for the next 155 days, the Cubs would occupy first place in the National League Eastern Division. Chicago was deliriously happy with Cubs Fever in anticipation of the North Siders' first World Series in twenty-four years.

And why not? On August 19, after pitcher Ken Holtzman's no-hitter, the Cubs led by eight-and-a-half games over the St. Louis Cardinals and nine-and-a-half over the New York Mets. On September 2, the Cubs still led by five games over the Mets with the Cardinals out of sight; but then the Cubs began an eight-game losing streak just as the Mets embarked on a ten-game winning streak.

The night the Mets moved into first place, September 11, saw Cub starting pitcher Dick Selma, whose cheerleading from the bullpen made him one of the team's most popular players that summer, call a pickoff play at third base against the Philadelphia Phillies. The signal for the pickoff attempt was "knock it down," and Selma yelled the phrase at third baseman Ron Santo.

Selma, confident that Santo would move to the bag, threw the ball to third. Santo was nowhere in sight. He had completely forgotten that "knock it down" was code for the pickoff play. The floodgates opened for a Phillies rally, and the Cubs lost both the game and first place. They would finish eight games behind the Mets. The media and a frantic fandom vilified Selma merely for calling a play that had been in the Cubs' arsenal all year.

At season's end, on October 3, the Cubs issued a statement, signed by all the players, that said how determined they were to make things right: "If you think that every man on this club will make every sacrifice in order to win in '70, you are correct. We have profited from our experience of the year and the mistakes that were a part of it. We wish the season were starting tomorrow so we could get on with our goal."[2]

The fans felt the same way.

2

WINTER OF CONTENTMENT

Looking at the Cubs' lineup after the 1969 season, fans had every reason to think that the 1970 edition could prove as good as or better than the 1969 club and that the team would fulfill its stated goal. The lineup still remained one of the strongest in baseball.

The infield consisted of future Hall of Famers Santo at third base and Ernie Banks at first, and All-Stars Don Kessinger, a switch-hitter, at shortstop and Glenn Beckert at second base. Banks needed only three more home runs to reach five hundred. All-Star Randy Hundley, who had introduced the one-handed catching style to the major leagues, was behind the plate, with youngster Ken Rudolph as his backup. Future Hall of Famer "Sweet Swingin'" Billy Williams played left field, and future All-Star and 1969 stretch-run star "Gentleman" Jim Hickman played right field.

Beckert also served as the team's jokester, keeping the other players relaxed and loose. "He was a funny guy," said Williams. "You just mention his name and I start laughing. He was quick-witted, too. He could come up with a whole bunch of stuff. He was just fun to be around."[3]

Starting pitching was superior, with a rotation of future Hall of Famer Ferguson Jenkins; Ken Holtzman, who in the early 1970s would become perhaps the best left-handed starting hurler in baseball; Bill "Froggy" Hands, who had won twenty games in 1969; and Selma, who had won twelve games with a nifty 3.68 earned run average (ERA).

The bullpen was equally stellar, with the two top National League relievers of the late 1960s. Phil "The Vulture" Regan had won twelve

Glenn Beckert was not only the Cubs' slick-fielding second baseman but the team's jokester as well. *National Baseball Hall of Fame Library.*

and saved seventeen for the Cubs in 1969, after leading the league in saves in 1966 and 1968. Regan had the reputation of moistening the ball to make his pitching more effective. In one 1968 game alone, umpire Chris Pelekoudas called fourteen illegal pitches on Regan, although the umpire never actually found any illegal substances on Regan or the ball. Because of the negative publicity this incident received, umpires toned down their searches for illegal substances on Regan, and he had a good year in 1969. Regan would be the last of the 1970 Cubs to wear a major-league uniform, serving as the New York Mets' pitching coach in 2019 at the age of eighty-two.

Ready to back him up was Ted Abernathy, who had led the league in saves in 1965 and 1967. Hank Aguirre was there to get the lefties out, and he had done so with a low 2.60 ERA in 1969. Abernathy and Aguirre often would warm up at the same time, to the tune of WGN-TV broadcaster Jack Brickhouse saying, "Ab and Ag in the bullpen." Rich Nye, a lefty who in 1967 and 1968 was a member of the Cubs' starting rotation, was there for long relief and for spot starts.

One or more rookie pitchers were expected to make the team. They included Jim Colborn, Jim Cosman, Joe Decker, Jim Dunegan, Larry Gura, Pat Jacquez, Dave Lemonds and Archie Reynolds. Pitching coach Joe Becker had wanted to retire after the 1969 season, "but his faith in his talented young pitching staff would not let him," according to the Cubs' 1970 roster book.[4] Even Manager Leo Durocher, usually no fan of rookies, was excited about the youngsters. "Leo liked what he saw at our Arizona Instructional Camp," said John Holland, vice-president and general manager.[5]

Reserve strength also was substantial, with Smith, the hero of Opening Day, who could play outfield or first base; Al Spangler, who had been the Cubs' starting right-fielder in early 1969; outfielder Jimmie Hall, one of the stars of the 1965 pennant-winning Minnesota Twins; and Paul Popovich, a slick glove man who could play any infield position.

The only questionable position was center field, where in 1969 the Cubs had rotated Don Young, Adolfo Phillips, Jimmy Qualls and Hall in an effort to find someone who could do the job every day. In August 1969, however, the team had already seemed to answer the question by bringing up nineteen-year-old rookie center fielder Oscar Gamble in time to play in the World Series that the Cubs would fail to make. Gamble started most of the Cubs' games in September, catching everything in sight, showing speed on the base paths and getting sixteen hits in twenty-four games.

Fan favorite Willie Smith led a strong Chicago Cub bench in 1970. *Chicago National League Ball Club Inc. (Chicago Cubs).*

The team's 1969 roster book noted that Gamble "has every chance of becoming the Ernie Banks of tomorrow."[6]

Manager Leo "The Lip" Durocher, long considered one of the game's best, had lost a little of his luster after ducking out of the July 26, 1969 Cub game, feigning illness but instead traveling to his stepson's boys' camp in Wisconsin, and after presiding over the Cubs' September swoon. Still, he had won a World Series with the New York Giants, as well as pennants with the Giants and the Brooklyn Dodgers, and he had taken a Cub team that had been moribund for twenty years and turned it into a contender.

Besides Becker, the coaching staff included returning coaches Verlon "Rube" Walker, and Joey Amalfitano, who coached at first base. Joining the Cubs as their third-base coach was Harry "Peanuts" Lowrey, who played in the World Series for the Cubs in 1945.

The nucleus of the team had been together for several years, and as Doug Feldmann wrote in his book *Miracle Collapse*, "it was obvious to those wearing the Cubs uniform that a sense of family had developed among the players" of that era. He quoted Jenkins as saying, "We were definitely close."[7]

Sure, the team had nearly won but failed the year before. But that was no reason they could not come back to finish first. Such a resurgence was nothing new in baseball history—even its recent history, and close to home, too. The Milwaukee Braves looked like they might win the National League pennant in both 1955 and 1956, only to finish second—but they won in both 1957 and 1958. The Chicago White Sox seemed poised to win the American League in 1957 and 1958 but also finished second—then won in 1959.

Banks had offered a cheerful slogan for every Cub season since 1967. "The Cubs will be heavenly in '67-ly." "The Cubs will be greater in '68-er." "The Cubs will shine in '69." For 1970, he assured fans, "The Cubs will go and glow in 7-0."

All in all, Cub fans could enjoy the glow of a winter of contentment. They knew that all Cub management had to do was stand pat, and the team would be fine.

Yet management could not refrain from making a good situation bad.

3
BROCK-FOR-BROGLIO REDUX

O ne of the major stories of the 1970 Cub season would be trades and acquisitions—some good, some questionable and some absolutely disastrous.

Number one in the disastrous category was the trade, on November 17, 1969, of nineteen-year-old Gamble, along with twenty-five-year-old starting pitcher Selma, to the Philadelphia Phillies for, as Steve Treder put it in the *Hardball Times*, "30-year-old fading star right fielder Johnny Callison."[8]

The Gamble-for-Callison trade was one in a long, depressing line of Cub trades of the 1960s and 1970s in which the team dealt a fast, young and Black player for an old, slow White one. The most infamous deal of course remains the Cubs trading Lou Brock to the St. Louis Cardinals for Ernie Broglio in 1964, but Gamble-for-Callison is not far behind. Nor is the Cub trade of Bill Madlock. After the 1976 season, the Cubs shipped the reigning two-time National League batting champion to the San Francisco Giants for past-his-prime outfielder Bobby Mercer. Madlock would go on to win two more batting championships after leaving the Giants for the Pittsburgh Pirates. Mercer achieved one good season for the Cubs in 1978 and was a New York Yankee by mid-1979. As far back as 1961, the Cubs traded Black right-fielder Lou Johnson straight up for White right-fielder Jim McAnany, who would go on to hit .188 for the Cubs. Johnson went on to be the star of the 1965 World Series for the Los Angeles Dodgers.

Were these trades truly race-based? Brock-for-Broglio certainly was. Lew Freedman, in his book *Ernie Banks: The Life and Career of "Mr. Cub,"* recounts

The trade of Oscar Gamble had dire consequences for the Cubs in 1970 and beyond. *SteveMooreArchives.photoshelter.com.*

that when Cub coach and scout Buck O'Neil objected to the idea of trading Brock, vice-president and general manager John Holland responded by showing O'Neil letters from Cubs season-ticket holders saying that the Cubs "were getting too black."[9]

Brock, of course, would go on to a Hall of Fame career with St. Louis and bat .391 with four home runs, sixteen RBI and fourteen steals in twenty-one World Series games, with thirteen hits in the 1968 World Series alone. The race-based Brock-for-Broglio deal was "what is generally considered the worst trade in baseball history."[10]

Gamble-for-Callison was a race-based trade, too—with dire consequences for the 1970 season and beyond.

When the Cubs called up the single, nineteen-year-old Gamble in late August 1969, he naturally started dating Chicago girls, "with many of his dates white women," according to Mitchell Nathanson in his book *A People's History of Baseball.*[11] Nathanson goes on to say that Cub manager Leo Durocher "insisted" that Gamble cease interracial dating, and when "Gamble refused, he was traded to Philadelphia."[12]

The Cubs had told Gamble he "was their center fielder for the next ten years."[13] Then they traded him. Edgar Munzel of the *Chicago Sun-Times* called Gamble "the best center field prospect the Cubs had."[14] Gamble would go on to put in seventeen solid seasons in the major leagues, be the top player on the 1977 "South Side Hit Men" Chicago White Sox and play in two World Series—neither with the Cubs, of course. Callison would hit a mediocre .264 with nineteen home runs for the Cubs in 1970, become a part-time player the next year and depart the team by 1972.

After the Cubs made the trade, Durocher tried to cover up the newly created and unnecessary hole in center field by telling the *Chicago Sun-Times,* "I might even try Callison there, if necessary." In the very same article, however, Callison responded by saying, "I can't run good enough for center."[15]

It would have been terrible enough for the Cubs to trade a future star for a fading star. It was even worse to trade their only center-field prospect for a right-fielder when, thanks to Hickman, nicknamed "The Guns of

August" in 1969 for his stellar late-season play, the team was set in right field. Then to make matters unbelievably worse, the Cubs "threw in" a starting pitcher in Selma, who had clearly worn out his welcome with the short-tempered Durocher merely due to his September pickoff attempt in Philadelphia.

The Cubs in 1970 would struggle the entire year with trying to find a bullpen ace, partially due to Regan having a bad season (five wins, nine losses, only twelve saves and a bulky ERA of 4.76), and partially due to the future disastrous trade of Abernathy. Selma could have been moved to the bullpen and become that ace. He was that ace in 1970 for the Philadelphia Phillies, who used him in relief in seventy-three games, with Selma winning eight and saving twenty-two (tying the Phillies' all-time save record) with a diminutive ERA of 2.75.

Years later, in discussing the baffling inclusion of Selma in the trade, Gamble asked, "Was he traded for messin' with some black girl?"[16]

With the departure of Gamble and Selma and the acquisition of Callison, a team that had no question marks suddenly had several. Who would play right field? If Callison, what would happen to Hickman? Who would play center field? Who would take the mound as the fourth starting pitcher?

The Cubs traded Dick Selma, one of their starting pitchers in 1969, to the Philadelphia Phillies in the offseason. Selma would prove to be the Phillies' top reliever in 1970. *Jewel-Osco.*

Putting Nye back in the starting pitching rotation was an obvious choice. He was only twenty-five, and a Cub rotation with two lefties, Holtzman and Nye, had already been a key reason for the team's 1967 ascent from wandering aimlessly in the second division for two decades to contender status.

It would take management less than three weeks from the Selma trade to subvert that plan with another less-than-stellar trade. On December 4, 1969, the Cubs traded Nye to the St. Louis Cardinals for center fielder Boots Day. How high was Durocher on Day? "Manager Leo Durocher announced the deal but immediately made it clear that he doesn't necessarily consider the 22-year-old Day the answer to the Cubs' center field problem," wrote Jerome Holtzman in the December 5 *Chicago Sun-Times*. "Asked if Day would be

Boots Day was one of several youngsters the Cubs traded for veterans in the early 1970s. After being shipped out to the Montreal Expos, he became their starting center fielder. *National Baseball Hall of Fame Library*.

the Wrigleys' No. 1 center field candidate, Durocher replied, 'No, he isn't. Nobody's No. 1.'"[17]

Day would play only eleven games for the 1970 Cubs, with just two hits and no extra-base hits or RBI, before being traded to the Montreal Expos on May 12 for Jack Hiatt. It was one of the Cubs' good trades of 1970. Hiatt led the Expos in hitting at the time, and for the Cubs he would often start at catcher in place of the frequently injured Randy Hundley that year.

Or was the trade that good? Day started in center field for the Expos for several years, batting .283 in 1971 and .275 in 1973. As for Hiatt, he put in a solid 1970 for the Cubs, but in December of that year, they sold him to the Houston Astros for cash, not even getting a player in return.

4

MARCH

IN LIKE A LION

In March, the U.S. Army pressed charges against fourteen officers concerning the My Lai massacre in Vietnam. The movie Airport *premiered. U.S. postal workers went on strike for the first time. Explorer 1, the first satellite ever launched by the United States, reentered Earth's atmosphere twelve years after its departure. And the Cubs went to spring training.*

After media and fans severely criticized Durocher in 1969 for constantly playing his regulars and starting three or four pitchers to the point of exhaustion, despite having a wealth of talent on the bench and in the bullpen, the manager came to spring training in Scottsdale, Arizona, with some new plans.

First, Durocher expected veterans to take mineral baths at Buckhorn Spa for a week for an extra bit of rejuvenation after a tiring 1969 season and long winter.

Second, business agents offering endorsement deals no longer would be allowed in the clubhouse. Many felt that such agents had hurt the Cubs' concentration on baseball in 1969.

Third, Durocher kicked around a new/old idea: a five-man starting rotation. As Edgar Munzel wrote in the *Chicago Sun-Times*, "Leo Durocher must find two starting pitchers to go along with his three aces"—Jenkins, Holtzman and Hands.[18]

Durocher came up to the majors with the New York Yankees in 1925; from 1922 to 1927, the Yanks led the American League in "five-man use every year, sometimes by large margins," according to Frank Vaccaro in the *Baseball Research Journal*.[19] Durocher had briefly considered a five-man rotation when spring training broke in 1969: Jenkins, Holtzman, Hands, Nye and Joe Niekro.[20] Unfortunately, he quickly fell into an even older pattern: Vaccaro points out that in 1969, Durocher used a style from the dead-ball era, a *three-man* rotation, thirty-six times.[21]

On March 7, rookies Larry Gura, Pat Jacquez and Jim Colborn combined to throw a 3–0 one-hitter against the California Angels. In 1970, although Durocher would not end up using the five-man rotation, he would not go back to burning out Jenkins, Holtzman and Hands with a three-man rotation for most of the season either (although he did still use the three-man through most of April). For much of the season, he ended up using a four-man rotation that would do quite well. During the regular season, Gura had three starts and Colborn five. Jacquez never made it to the big club.

Typical of those years, Gura and Colborn later became stars with other clubs after the Cubs let them go in questionable trades. In 1973, they traded Gura to the Texas Rangers for pitcher Mike Paul, 0-2 for the Cubs in 1973 and 1974 and out of baseball in 1975. Gura went on to pitch in five playoffs and one World Series for the Kansas City Royals, winning eighteen games in 1980 and eighteen again in 1982. The Cubs traded Colborn and two other players to the Milwaukee Brewers for José Cardenal, who did have some great years in Chicago. However, in 1973, Colborn won twenty games for the Brewers in a year when no Cub pitcher would win more than fourteen.

Two days before the three rookie pitchers' gem, Durocher announced how he would solve the Cubs' right field/center field problem. Callison would start in right—how could he not after the Cubs had traded Gamble and Selma for him?—and Hickman would start in center field despite his limited speed and range, to get Gentleman Jim's big bat in the lineup. Durocher planned to spell Hickman in center occasionally with Day, an experiment that lasted only a short time, as Day would play only eleven games in center field before being traded on May 12.

The *Sun-Times*' Munzel wrote that a "mild surprise was Durocher's naming of Hickman as the center field starter….He hadn't given Jim much attention and had said he wanted to look first at his rookie center field candidates."[22]

One of those rookies was Jimmy McMath, who had played in six games for the Cubs in 1968; however, the U.S. Army drafted him as the Vietnam War continued to rage during spring training 1970, and he never played in the major leagues again. Another was Cleo James, who had only ten games under his belt for the 1968 Los Angeles Dodgers.

Durocher eventually fell into a pattern beginning in May of starting Hickman in center field, bringing in James late in the game as a defensive replacement and moving Hickman to first to provide better late-inning defense than the aging Banks could provide. Durocher also started James in center field a number of times, particularly at midseason, when the manager decided to go with a lineup that featured James starting in center and Hickman at first. James served as the Cubs' super sub in 1970, playing in one hundred games. With Cleon Jones already playing for the New York Mets, when Cleo James made the Cubs, WGN-TV broadcaster Jack Brickhouse said, "This is going to be confusing."

The rookie whom Durocher finally settled on as Selma's replacement was Joe Decker, who in a late September 1969 call-up from the minor leagues was the only Cub pitcher to beat the New York Mets that month. Decker would start seventeen games and hurl more than one hundred innings in 1970. He looked particularly impressive combining with Bill Hands on a three-hit 4–0 shutout of the Seattle Pilots late in spring training on March 25, days before the Pilots would become the Milwaukee Brewers. Decker would end up pitching eleven scoreless innings that spring.

Decker would not prove the answer for the Cubs in 1970 but, of course, would prove the answer for another team subsequently. The Cubs would eventually trade Decker—along with starting pitcher Hands—to the Minnesota Twins after the 1972 season, and Decker would immediately move into the Twins' starting rotation, winning sixteen games in 1974— more than any Cub starter that year. Trading two starting pitchers for a reliever, Dave LaRoche, who would post ERAs of 5.80 in 1973 and 4.79 in 1974 for the Cubs before being dealt away to Cleveland, was yet another trade in which another team took Cub management to the cleaners. Twins catcher George Mitterwald would later say that Decker "has more stuff than any pitcher I've ever caught."[23]

Durocher in the *Sun-Times* on April 5 suggested that Colborn would serve as the fifth starter.[24]

The Cubs on March 24 released two veterans who had been with the team all year in 1969: outfielder Al Spangler and catcher Bill Heath. Spangler would go to the minors and return to the Cubs later in the season. Heath, who had caught Holtzman's no-hitter in 1969, would never play in the majors again.

Had Heath been able to hang on for a couple more days, however, he might have looked more valuable. The Cubs suddenly had another question mark when, on March 26, catcher Hundley suffered a chip fracture of his

Cub management made a surprising deal at the end of spring training by acquiring veteran catcher J.C. Martin from the New York Mets, the Cubs' biggest rivals. *National Baseball Hall of Fame Library.*

left thumb when catcher Dave Duncan of the Oakland Athletics slid into Hundley in a play at the plate, putting him out of action for at least ten days.

Management then made the first of its surprising good deals of 1970, on March 29 trading rookie catcher Randy Bobb to the Mets for veteran catcher J.C. Martin, whose tenth-inning bunt had won Game Four of the previous year's World Series for New York. Bobb would never play in the majors again, and bringing a player so identified with the team's biggest rival as Martin was showed that Cub management was willing to actually think outside of the box when making a deal. Youngster Ken Rudolph would serve as the second backup catcher.

Martin paid immediate dividends on April 2, going two-for-four, and on April 3, going two-for-five with a grand slam, as spring training wound down. The Cubs would finish the spring with a 19-10 record—second best in all of baseball.

Despite the spa treatment, winning spring and talk about how the Cubs would be more relaxed in 1970, Santo on March 29 showed the pressure the Cubs *already* felt by challenging a heckler to come down on the field and then going after the fan. "It took a half dozen of his mates to pull him back down from the railing," Munzel wrote of Santo in the *Sun-Times*. "The police then moved in and ejected the heckler. Oddly enough, he bought a Cub cap on the way out."[25]

Cub vice-president John Holland inadvertently confirmed that feeling of pressure in the same article, talking about the Martin trade. "We're at the point now where many of our stars are at their peak," Holland said. "It's now or never."[26]

5

APRIL

SHOWERS OF WINS

In April, President Richard Nixon signed the Public Health Cigarette Smoking Act, banning TV cigarette advertising starting seven months later. Paul McCartney announced the breakup of the Beatles. The Apollo 13 space capsule suffered an explosion in space, but the astronauts returned safely. America held the first Earth Day. And the Cubs began regular-season play.

Despite feeling the pressure, the Cubs, Durocher, the fans and the media also felt confident. Munzel of the *Sun-Times* wrote on April 5: "I'm not yet convinced the Cubs didn't have the best ball club in the National League last year, and this season I believe they'll prove it.... It is our conviction, without benefit of any computers, that it will be the Cubs in the East and the Reds in the West, and then the Cubs will take it all in the playoffs."[27] Rick Talley of the *Chicago Today* newspaper went even further, calling the Cubs "the best team in baseball" and writing that at the end of the season, "you'll find a world championship banner whipping in the breeze above Wrigley Field."[28]

Yet the headline writers for both papers subconsciously showed the nagging fear of how 1970 might turn out by using negative language. Psychologists, linguists and religious thinkers have long noted that "words that are negative" can create "fears and self-doubt. Words have a way of working into our subconscious mind. They linger there waiting."[29] The *Sun-Times*' headline "Cubs Won't Collapse" and the *Today*'s headline "No Cub Slump in 'Year of Power'" manifested many people's subconscious fears.

In 1970, the exterior of Wrigley Field had no statues and few fan amenities, and the roof had no lights. Some, however, predicted that the park would host a World Series championship banner at the end of the season. *Chicago History Museum, ICHi-024209; John Spiro, photographer.*

The first slump came immediately as the Phillies shut out the Cubs, 2–0, with only five hits on Opening Day, April 7, in Philadelphia. The Cubs lost the next game against Philadelphia, 5–3; James came in as a late-inning defensive replacement for Hickman for the first of many times that year. The Cubs then moved along to Montreal. In the third game of the season, they trailed the Expos, 1–0, in the ninth inning, when Santo singled and Callison homered to eke out the team's first win. They then lost another lackluster performance against the second-year Expos before coming home to Chicago.

Whereupon Talley's "best team in baseball" finally showed up.

The home opener on April 14 had field announcer Pat Peiper declare, as he had done since 1916, "Have your pencils, and scorecards ready, and we'll give you the correct lineup for today's ballgame." In that era, the bleacher seats and all grandstand seats—more than 22,400 in total—went on sale the day of the game instead of ahead of time. Team owner Phil

Wrigley believed, as he had since he took over the team in 1932, that people ought to have the opportunity to wake up in the morning and decide that day to go to the game.

The outfield walls were covered with a combination of Japanese bittersweet and Boston ivy, as they had since 1937, and the center-field bleachers were covered with Astroturf, as they had been since 1967, to provide a better visual backdrop for hitters. There were still "catwalks" instead of seats and scoreboards between the foul poles and the bleachers. Wrigley Field had no lights, so the Cubs played all day games.

After the financially successful 1969 season, Cub management spent $750,000 on sprucing up Wrigley Field over the winter, replacing 7,500 seats in both the upper and lower decks, rebuilding part of the lower deck grandstand, getting rid of the last folding-chair box seats and reconstructing the upper deck from home plate toward right field.[30]

Down the left-field line stood a chain-link fence at the end of the grandstand, and the Cubs still allowed people to put up slogans like "Cubs #1" spelled out in beer and pop cups stuck into the fence. Kids also liked to turn a cup upside-down on the concrete and stomp on it; if you did it just right, the popping sound reverberated around the park.

The center field bleachers were covered with Astroturf, as they had been since 1967, to provide a better visual backdrop for hitters. The turf seat covering was removed after the 1996 season. *William S. Bike.*

Cub regulars take batting practice before a game. Billy Williams is in the batting cage, Ernie Banks is to the left talking to media, Jim Hickman is to the right of the cage and Ron Santo is two players to the right of Hickman. Left field still featured a "catwalk" between the box seats and bleachers. *William S. Bike.*

In that era, the Cubs gave free tickets to future games to kids who would flip up the old-fashioned wooden seats after a game. "I saw most of the games for free—imagine that!—because I stayed after the game and put up the seats in an entire row from left to right field so maintenance people could come through with a broom and clean up," recalled Ken Hennig, who as a youngster lived near Wrigley Field. "Sometimes they would have us go on the warning track and clean up trash from the bleachers. In 1969, I saw 49 games, most through flipping up seats."[31]

Rooftops across Waveland and Sheffield Avenues were just that—rooftops, with no permanent seats on them, and the buildings were residential, not sports clubs. A handful of residents of the buildings would take their lawn chairs up on the roofs and enjoy the games. One of the rooftops on Sheffield had a Schlitz beer sign, and the oddly shaped roof across the street on Waveland Avenue with the cone-like tower sported an advertisement for WGN-TV Channel 9.

An official game program cost fifteen cents and featured an artist's rendering of a Cub infielder turning a double-play. Artist Otis Shepard pioneered the classic Cubs' program artistic style in the 1940s; when he retired after drawing the 1963 program cover, another artist drew program covers in Shepard's style through 1972.

Yosh Kawano, who joined the Cubs in the late 1940s, remained as the team's clubhouse manager, and the team paid batboys ten dollars per game. Music during the game came from a real organ and organist; the Cubs installed a new organ over the winter of 1969–70. The Chicago Bears football team still played at Wrigley in the fall and winter. (Wrigley Field at one time held the record for football games played at a stadium with 344.) The neighborhood was not a popular tourist destination then; it was just a regular Chicago residential neighborhood.

Entertainer Milton Berle was the master of ceremonies for the home opener, and he led the crowd in prayer for the return of the Apollo 13 astronauts, who were in danger after an oxygen tank in their service module exploded in outer space. The crew eventually safely returned to Earth.

Cub radio broadcaster Lou Boudreau threw out the first ball to Cub Hall-of-Famer Gabby Hartnett.

Hundley was healed and back in the lineup against the Phillies, and the Cubs wore new, bolder logos on their uniforms. The team's hitting finally came around as Cub batters banged out twelve hits and the team won, 5–4. That Phillies series saw the oddity of Selma both pitching and playing third base on April 16, a day when Hundley went three-for-five with the game-winning RBI.

Selma already waxed nostalgic about playing in Chicago. Whenever he and the Phillies came to town that year, he and some Philadelphia

On April 16 against the Philadelphia Phillies, Randy Hundley went three-for-five with the game-winning RBI. More valuable to the Cubs than Hundley's bat, however, was his ability as a catcher to get the best out of Cub pitchers. *National Baseball Hall of Fame Library.*

teammates after the games would stop into a bar behind Wrigley Field at Waveland and Sheffield Avenues, Ray's Bleachers (now Murphy's Bleachers), to visit with Cub fans.

The Cubs swept the series against both the Phillies and the Expos; in the April 18 game against Montreal, pitcher Ken Johnson held the Cubs scoreless for two innings. Veteran Johnson had been a Cub in late 1969, winning a game and saving another down the stretch, but the Cubs had released him at the beginning of the 1970 season. He was the first of several relievers on whom the Cubs had given up but who could have played a role later in the season when the team sought a closer.

Next, the Cardinals came to town. The Cubs swept that series, too, but disaster struck in the first game, April 21, when Hundley again suffered an injury in another play at the plate. The umpire called the Cards' Carl Taylor out at home after he slid into Hundley, who tore a ligament in his left knee and required a cast for several weeks and physical therapy thereafter. Cardinal manager Red Schoendienst grumbled about the out call, noting of Hundley, "He hasn't tagged him yet."[32]

That 7–4 victory put the Cubs into a tie for first place, and their seventh victory in a row, a 7–5 win over the Cardinals on April 22, the first Earth Day, both swept the St. Louis series and vaulted the Cubs into sole possession of first place. That same day, the Cubs brought Gura up

In April, the Cubs signed former Baltimore Oriole Steve Barber, the first of several surprising acquisitions of players who had gotten in trouble in other organizations. *National Baseball Hall of Fame Library.*

to the big club from their Tacoma farm club, and they traded Jim Qualls, one of their 1969 platoon of center fielders, to Montreal for infielder Garry Jestadt, who, after a 1971 trade to the San Diego Padres for catcher Chris Canizzaro, would serve as the Padres' starting shortstop that year and the next.

The Cubs also signed veteran free agent left-handed pitcher Steve Barber, the first of several surprising acquisitions of players who had gotten in trouble in other organizations— the type of player from whom the Cubs usually shied away. Society for American Baseball Research writer Warren Corbett described Barber, a former twenty-game winner with the Baltimore Orioles, as having "a chip on his shoulder....Barber was wild after hours as well."[33]

An eleven-game Cub winning streak included an 11–5 victory over Houston in which Ernie Banks hit a home run off *Ball Four* author Jim Bouton. *National Baseball Hall of Fame Library*.

The Cubs sent him to triple-A Tacoma before bringing him up to the big club on May 14. He lasted only a month and a half with the team, leaving with an 0-1 record and a 9.53 ERA.

The Houston Astros were the next victims to come to Chicago. The Cubs' eighth victory in a row, a 6–3 win, saw the first-ever Wrigley Field appearance of Joe Pepitone, for Houston. "Pepi" would play a key role for the Cubs later in the season. The Yankees had traded Pepitone to the Astros over the winter.

Number nine in the winning streak saw the Cubs score in double digits for the first time in the season in an 11–5 April 25 victory, one in which Ernie Banks hit his 498th career home run off Jim Bouton of the Astros. Bouton, who would go from obscure pitcher to notorious author later in the year thanks to the June publication of one of the first tell-all baseball books, *Ball Four*, started the game for Houston. The umpire called him out at a play at the plate in the second inning, in which he unsuccessfully threw a "football block into Martin, hoping to knock the ball loose."[34]

A day later, the Cubs ended the home stand with a 6–3 victory, a perfect 10-0 record at home an 11-3 record overall. They were in first place with a two-game lead over the Cardinals and the Pirates. Cub Power was alive and well, as the team never scored less than five runs in any game during the home stand.

Joe Decker took the mound for his first start of the year in Pittsburgh and hurled the best game he would pitch in 1970, blanking the Pirates for eight and one-third innings before yielding to Aguirre and Regan, who preserved the 1–0 shutout, running the winning streak to eleven. The Cubs scored their lone run on an odd play, with Beckert hitting what looked like an inside-the-park home run in spacious Forbes Field, only to have the scorer rule the play a triple and an error on catcher Manny Sanguillen.

So, on April 27, the Cubs stood at 12-3, a start so hot it would not be matched by any Cub team until 2020.

The Pirates ended the streak the next night, winning 6–1 on two Sanguillen home runs, but the Cubs came right back the night after with a 10–5 victory in which the lights in old Forbes went out for a while.

The last April game was a 9–2 loss to the Braves in Atlanta. Notable in the game was left-fielder Billy Williams becoming the first player in National League history to play in one thousand straight games. Also notable was the unusual situation of Milt Pappas, one of the Braves' pitchers, seeking out Durocher during batting practice to let the manager know that Atlanta was not using him and that he was available should the Cubs want him.[35]

April had been the cruelest month to the Cubs' opponents, but it had been good to them. The team had the best record it would achieve in any month in 1970, going 13-5 for a .722 winning percentage and a two-and-a-half game hold on first place.

In 1969, the Bleacher Bums had been a happy bunch of Wrigley Field fans, enjoying the sunshine and gently taunting the opposition. During the April 1970 home stand, a different type of fan came to Wrigley, as opposed to the fun-loving Bums. As Jim Langford described the situation in his book *The Game Is Never Over*, "gangs of rowdies were roaming through the stands, starting fights, throwing debris on the field, and jumping over outfield walls, interrupting play."[36]

Phil Wrigley, owner of the Cubs, immediately after the home stand ordered significant changes to retain the "Beautiful Wrigley Field" ambiance he had worked so hard to create over the decades. Management hired more and tougher security personnel and issued them walkie-talkies for the first time; added Chicago Police patrols on some days; installed security cameras in the bleachers; and posted signs spelling out: "Spectators forbidden to enter or throw objects on playing field. Violators will be prosecuted."

Workers mortared concrete triangles onto the formerly flat tops of the outfield walls so rowdies could no longer walk on the walls and jump onto the field. To make doubly sure that people stayed in the seats, Cub management added the "basket"—wire netting angling out at a forty-five-degree angle from two and a half feet below the top of the wall to catch both thrown trash and possible jumpers. No longer did the Cubs need to send kids on the field after the game to pick up trash thrown from the bleachers.

The basket, a fixture in Wrigley Field to this day, was therefore an almost unheard-of midseason change to the dimensions of a major-league field, effectively reducing the distance from home plate by about thirty inches. Fans hoped that when Ernie Banks hit his five hundredth home run, it would not be a "cheapie" in the basket.

Problems caused by some at Wrigley Field indicated increasing cynicism and frustration in America at the time. For society in general, once President Richard Nixon dashed hopes for a quick end to the Vietnam War after he took office, Americans' moods darkened as the 1970s began.

Yet Wrigley Field generally remained an exuberant place because of the composition of the crowd. Because of the economical prices (bleacher and kids' tickets cost only $1.00, even lower-deck box seats cost only $3.50, soft drinks cost $0.15 and $0.25, popcorn also cost $0.15 and a hot dog cost $0.35); frequent Ladies' Days, a fixture at Wrigley Field since 1919 in which the Cubs admitted girls and women age fourteen and older for free; and owner Phil Wrigley's devotion to Beautiful Wrigley Field/the Friendly Confines as family friendly, crowds were young and zealous and sat close together in a park with a capacity of 36,667. On Tuesdays, the Cubs admitted seniors at a reduced cost, and the older crowd showed plenty of enthusiasm as well.

Once school let out in May or June, attendance increased and the average age of fans decreased. Even when school remained in session, Wednesday attendance often was larger, as many children attending Roman Catholic grade schools in Chicago had Wednesday afternoons off so that public school kids could have catechism classes at the Catholic schools. Since the Cubs played only day games at Wrigley, it provided a great place for moms to take kids for a few hours of economical entertainment. Virtually every time a Cub bat made contact with a ball, the swing was met with screams of anticipation from young voices, seldom heard in the major leagues in the twenty-first century, as fewer kids attend. In 1970, fans at the park and those listening on TV and radio could hear thousands of child Cub fans cheering on their heroes throughout the summer.

6

MAY

MEDIOCRITY

In May, President Nixon ordered U.S. forces to invade Cambodia. Three days later, Ohio State National Guard troops at Kent State University shot at students protesting the invasion, killing four and wounding nine. The New York Knicks won the National Basketball Association championship. And the Cubs started the month in first place by two and a half games

Don't let the highs get too high or the lows get too low. This is an axiom in both sports and life, and one criticism of the 1969 Cubs was that they did just that. An early May game in Atlanta showed that, despite promises to the contrary, their up-and-down attitude had not changed very much since the previous year.

Despite their astonishing April, a mere two straight losses to the Braves in Atlanta on April 30 and May 1 had the team on edge. In the sixth inning of the May 2 game, with Braves batter Pat Jarvis nursing a two-and-two count, he checked his swing on the next pitch. Plate umpire Harry Wendelstedt called it a ball. Cub catcher Martin asked for a ruling from first-base umpire Tony Venson, who confirmed Wendelstedt's no-swing/ball call.

Such an occurrence happens in baseball all the time, but in this instance, Durocher shot out of the dugout to argue with Venson, first mimicking Venson's no-swing body language and then giving Venson the finger—whereupon Venson immediately threw Durocher out of the game. Durocher returned to the dugout, but before departing, he continued giving Venson the finger, "recorded on television (WGN-TV) for the enlightenment of all the folks back in Chicago."[37]

Jack Brickhouse, who broadcast the Cubs from 1948 to 1981, observed that the team had particular difficulties on the road in 1970. *National Baseball Hall of Fame Library*.

With the count three-and-two on Jarvis, Wendelstedt called Cub hurler Holtzman's next pitch ball four, causing Holtzman to charge off the mound and scream at the umpire. Wendelstedt then ejected Holtzman, who mimicked the umpire by pretending to eject Wendelstedt with Holtzman's own thumb.

All in all, it was an overreaction to a standard baseball situation. The Cubs lost that game, the league suspended Durocher for a day and the team lost the next two at Houston and the May 7 game back at Wrigley Field as well, for a sudden six-game losing streak—the first five of which had come on the road.

As Cubs/WGN-TV broadcaster Jack Brickhouse frequently said in those years, "The road is a jungle for the Cubs."

They remained in first place, however.

From May 8 through 19, the Cubs had a mediocre stretch, going 3-3 at home and 2-3 on the road.

The May 8 slump-buster was a 10–7 win over the Reds that featured four home runs by the Cubs—two from Williams and one each from Hickman and Martin—and four by the Reds. In an 8–1 laugher the next day, Banks hit career home run number 499 on to Waveland Avenue. But two 7–6 losses,

The Cubs-Reds series of May 8–10, 1970, drew a large crowd to Wrigley Field, which still had a catwalk and no scoreboard in right field. *Blake Bolinger.*

one against the Reds on a Pete Rose home run and one against the Atlanta Braves in ten innings, followed.

In the May 10 loss to the Reds, Banks hit a triple and was tempted to continue on to home before deciding to hold up at third. Had he made it all the way around the bases, his five hundredth homer incredibly would have been an inside-the-park job.

Despite having come up with some big hits, catcher Martin was hitting only .167, and Hundley was still undergoing therapy after having the cast removed from his knee. To obtain some quick punch from the catcher's position, the Cubs traded Day to Montreal for veteran catcher Jack Hiatt, who was hitting .326 for the Expos. He would end up being the Cubs' regular starting catcher for much of the season, playing in only seven fewer games than Hundley.

Hiatt arrived for one of the highlights of the season on Tuesday, May 12, when Ernie Banks hit his five-hundredth home run—Banks jacked it into the bleachers, not the basket. At the time, that made him only the ninth player to achieve that mark. A typical early season weekday crowd of only 5,264 witnessed the historic blast, which came against the Atlanta Braves.

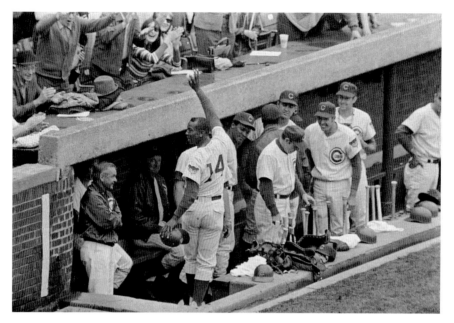

After hitting his five-hundredth home run in the second inning of the Cubs' May 12, 1970 game against the Atlanta Braves, Ernie Banks turns toward the fans and acknowledges the applause. *AP Photo/Jim Palmer.*

The pitcher was Pat Jarvis. The count was one ball, one strike. Jack Brickhouse called it: "Jarvis fires away. That's a fly ball, deep to left, back, back, hey! He did it! Ernie Banks got number 500! The ball tossed to the bullpen. Everybody on your feet. This is it! Wheee!"[38]

Banks's teammates mobbed him at home plate after the homer, the only one he hit off Jarvis in his career.

Coming off a span in which the Cubs had lost eight of their last ten games, the team initially continued to look lackluster that day. Down 2-0 when Banks hit his homer in the second inning and still losing 3-1 in the seventh, the team got it together to rally and score in the seventh and ninth innings, when Williams hit a home run to tie the game, and won it in the eleventh when Ron Santo singled in Don Kessinger with the winning run.

As a promotion, the Cubs offered the fan who caught the historic blast $250, a season's pass to Wrigley Field and a night on the town with Banks. High school student Jim McEnerny was closest to the line drive when it hit the concrete in the second row and bounced out onto the field. Braves' left-fielder Rico Carty retrieved it, and he gave the ball to Willie Smith in the

Cubs' bullpen to forward it to Banks. "I muffed it," said McEnerny.[39] The Cubs instead gave the $250 to the Purple Heart Cruise, an annual outing for disabled veterans run by *Sun-Times* columnist Irv Kupcinet.

Banks, who always wanted to "play two," really did not want to leave Wrigley Field that day, enjoying every interview and staying until after 6:00 p.m., even sweeping one of the aisles and helping a groundskeeper water the field.[40]

The Cubs looked dismal in their first 1970 meeting with the hated New York Mets at Wrigley the very next day on May 13, as Mets' pitcher Gary Gentry ungently threw a one-hitter against the Cubs and won, 4–0. The lone Chicago hit came from Banks in the eighth inning, snatching a no-hitter from Gentry late in the game just as Qualls had done against the Mets' Tom Seaver a year before. The box score in the *Sun-Times* the next day referred to Banks's two-day adventure as "Hero to Villain," bringing the newspaper criticism from fans who did not know that sportswriters at the time typically used "villain" as a reference for a player who broke up a no-hitter.

After the rain canceled the second scheduled game against the Mets, the Cubs hit the road, winning one of three in St. Louis and splitting a two-game series in Cincinnati. In the Cubs' 3–2 May 16 victory, pitcher Ken Holtzman got the game-winning RBI against St. Louis with a fifth-inning double. Cub reliever Abernathy hit Cardinal batter Dick Allen in the head with a wicked submarine pitch.

Cub ace Ferguson Jenkins was actually having a bad season up to this point, and the Cardinals beat him on May 17, with Jenkins falling to 2-6 with a 4.82 ERA. The next day's *Sun-Times* headline read, "Fergie Fails Again, Cubs Fade 4–3," and the box score headline read, "Fergie Flop."

The team then split two games in Cincinnati, the Cubs' last appearance in Crosley Field. The Cubs had been the Reds' first opponents at Crosley when the park opened on April 11, 1912.

The Cubs then headed back to Chicago for their annual exhibition game against the Chicago White Sox in Comiskey Park on May 21. Durocher tried a couple of interesting experiments, starting All-Star second baseman Beckert in center field and Banks at shortstop for the first time in several years. Hickman powered a home run that hit a light tower on the left-field roof, and the Cubs won, 7–6.

There had been talk for two years about the White Sox leaving town because of poor attendance in the South Side neighborhood in which they played, but the game drew a healthy crowd of 28,863. "That should diminish those silly arguments about the kind of neighborhood in which the White Sox live," the *Sun-Times'* Jerome Holtzman wrote. "Nobody was mugged, assaulted, or even pursued."[41]

The game also saw a blond female fan decide to sit in the Cub dugout around mid-contest, until umpire John Rice sent her back into the stands.

That day, Cub management learned that Hundley's knee was hurt worse than anyone had thought, because previously unseen cartilage damage required immediate surgery. Hundley would spend two months on the disabled list, and Hiatt became the regular catcher.

Hiatt would have a decent season, but the loss of Hundley was a blow. Hundley was much more valuable than his .226 and .255 batting averages of the previous two years indicated. According to the *Sun-Times*, "He's the guy who can drive Ferguson Jenkins when Fergie starts to ease off, and he gets more out of the kid pitchers than they know they have."[42]

Jenkins himself agreed: "Having Hundley catch for you was like sitting down to a steak dinner with a steak knife. Without Hundley, all you had was a fork."[43] It is small wonder that Jenkins had been struggling at that point of the season.

With the Cubs' first-place record at a modest 18-16 and a half-game lead over the Mets, the team rolled into New York for a four-game weekend series against the World Series champions that had Cub fans worried.

They need not have been concerned. A 6–4 Friday-night May 22 Cub victory started the weekend off right, with a 14–8 laugher the next day. Hands beat the Mets' Tom Seaver 3–1 in the opener of the Sunday doubleheader, before the Mets finally salvaged the nightcap. The Cubs' great weekend had put the Mets in third place and under .500, with the Cardinals in second.

With that confidence-building weekend under their belts, the Cubs came back to Wrigley for a homestand that would see female ushers for the first time since the 1940s, and they took two of three from Pittsburgh (with Jenkins dropping to 3-7 with a 5.01 ERA in a 4–0 May 27 loss).

The Cubs acquired the Montreal Expos' leading hitter, Jack Hiatt, in May, and he became the Cubs' starting catcher for much of the season. *National Baseball Hall of Fame Library.*

May 29 saw the Cubs make their second disastrous, pennant-losing deal of the year when they traded relief pitcher Ted Abernathy, who would later become one of the top relievers of 1970 with the Kansas City Royals. *National Baseball Hall of Fame Library.*

The next day, Hickman, who had hit two walk-off home runs in five days in 1969, picked up where he left off the year before, hitting two homers and a two-run walk-off to beat the Pirates, 8–7.

May 29 saw the Cubs make their second disastrous, pennant-losing trade of the year when they traded relief pitcher Ted Abernathy to the St. Louis Cardinals for reserve infielder Phil Gagliano. Cub fans were distraught at Ag losing his Ab, as the bullpen duo of Aguirre and Abernathy had been reduced by half.

With the Gamble-for-Callison deal, one can at least see the race-based reason for it, abhorrent as that reason was. To this day, the Abernathy-for-Gagliano trade remains inexplicable, other than the fact that Durocher asked for it despite the manager having told Abernathy in spring training that the submariner would pitch more than the previous year, according to David Claerbaut in his book *Durocher's Cubs.*[44]

At 2.00, Abernathy's ERA was lower than that of Regan, the Cubs' usual closer. In fact, Durocher had just used Abernathy as the closer in the May 27 game. Abernathy had led the league in saves in both 1965 and 1967 and in games pitched in 1965, 1967 and 1968. His unusual submarine delivery had thrown hitters off-balance for more than a decade, and that made him an ideal candidate for either set-up man or closer.

Gagliano, on the other hand, simply was not needed. The Cubs already had super sub Paul Popovich, who could play any infield position. Cub management wanted another infielder, because Kessinger was scheduled for a couple of weeks of military duty in June, but they already had Jestadt and Nate Oliver in the minor leagues. Oliver had been with the big club all of 1969 and was a particular fan favorite. Gagliano, hitting only .187 when the Cubs acquired him, would play in only twenty-six games for the Cubs in 1970 and bat an appalling .150.

Before 1970 ended, the Cubs shipped Gagliano to the Boston Red Sox for Carmen Fanzone. Gagliano had a couple of good years coming off the bench for Boston, and Fanzone became a fan favorite for the Cubs in the early 1970s, playing both infield for the Cubs and trumpet in various clubs around Chicago. But that did not help them in 1970.

When Regan faltered later in the year, the Cubs, with varying degrees of success, tried Roberto Rodriguez, Juan Pizarro, Hoyt Wilhelm and others as possible closers. Abernathy would have been the ideal candidate to fill the bill. Instead, after a month in St. Louis, Abernathy ended up as the closer for the Kansas City Royals, winning nine games and saving twelve with a 2.59 ERA in 1970. He had another stellar bullpen year for Kansas City in 1971, pitching in sixty-three games, winning four and saving twenty-three, with a 2.56 ERA.

Durocher did not appreciate Abernathy's unique underhand delivery—the exact attribute that made Abernathy a top reliever. "He's almost impossible to hit when you get only one shot at him," read the Kansas City Royals' 1971 Yearbook.[45]

Problems caused by the departure of Abernathy would not become apparent until later in the season, however.

To close out the month, the Cubs took two of three from the San Diego Padres, with game one of the Saturday, May 30 doubleheader marking the Padres' first-ever victory in the Friendly Confines. In the 11–4 loss, Hickman hit a three-run homer in the third inning, his sixth in the last eight games, and rookie Jim Dunegan was the losing pitcher.

Jim Hickman, who would have his best major-league season in 1970, had a stretch of six home runs in eight games in late May. *Chicago National League Ball Club Inc. (Chicago Cubs).*

Before game two, which the Cubs won, 8–7, the team honored Banks and Williams, with Cub owner Philip K. Wrigley establishing college scholarships for Williams's four children and Banks's three and providing the two stars with checks for postseason family vacations. The Cubs also gave donations to La Rabida Children's Hospital in Banks's name and to Mobile Training School in Williams's name. Retailer Montgomery Ward provided $500 to donate to a kids' baseball league in Banks's name, and the Hillerich and Bradsby Co., makers of the Louisville Slugger bat, provided Banks with a silver-plated bat to honor his five-hundredth home run.

Jenkins was the Fergie of the last three years, as he went nine innings in beating the Padres, 7–4, on May 31.

The Cubs ended May in first place by two games over the Mets. Kessinger and Hickman were hitting over .300, Beckert and Williams each were above .285, Hands was 7-2 and Holtzman was 6-3. The biggest concerns were the absence of Hundley, Jenkins's slow start and Regan's 4.02 ERA—high for a closer in those days.

JUNE

AN UNWELCOME SWOON

In June, the federal Voting Rights Act Amendment of 1970 went into effect, giving eighteen-year-olds the right to vote. Baseball commissioner Bowie Kuhn reprimanded the Houston Astros' Jim Bouton for writing the book Ball Four. *Edwin Land received a patent for the Polaroid camera. Chicago Bears running back Brian Piccolo passed away. About thirty Native Americans set up a "community of occupation" near Wrigley Field to protest inferior housing conditions. And the Cubs started the month in first place by two games.*

As the month began, the Cubs looked good. Continuing the long, eleven-game home stand, the Cubs split a two-game series against Los Angeles, losing 5–4 and winning 6–5, both without Banks. This series marked the beginning of Banks becoming a part-time player for the first time in his career, as the first baseman's ailing knees caused Durocher to sit him down in favor of Smith or Hickman at first. With Hickman usually at first, James became the Cubs' regular center fielder.

In the top of the eleventh in the June 3 game, with the Dodgers threatening, Los Angeles batter José Peña snuffed out the Dodger rally on an odd play in which he interfered with the catcher and became the third out instead of getting on base. The Cubs won it, 6–5, when Hickman singled in Beckert in the bottom of the frame.

The next day, June 4, was the 1970 Major League Baseball draft, and the Cubs in the third round chose Rick Reuschel, who would become their top pitcher in the late 1970s and a member of their 1984 division-winning club.

Left: Ernie Banks's ailing knees resulted in him spending less time in the field and becoming a part-time player for the first time. *Photo 112145772 © Sports Images/Dreamstime.com.*

Right: Cleo James, who had regularly come in for late-inning defense early in the season, became the Cubs' starting center fielder in June. *National Baseball Hall of Fame Library.*

The Cubs then took two of three from the Giants, with the suddenly rejuvenated Jenkins beating Juan Marichal in a 12–8 June 5 slugfest, a scoring total unusual when the two Hall of Famers took the mound. The home stand–closing 8–4 victory of June 7 saw the Cubs hit five home runs. Popovich, not Gagliano, took over at shortstop as Kessinger went off to spend a few days in the military reserves—a situation typical in that era, when about one hundred of the six hundred major leaguers served in the military reserves, making them eligible for military call-up for a time in the summer. A *New York Times* article that day, "Military Call-Ups May Decide Major League Pennant Races," prominently featured Kessinger's call-up to the reserves.[46]

Next came a West Coast swing, normally a minefield for the Cubs, but the hot club took two of three games in each series against the Padres, Dodgers and Giants.

With Billy Williams having such a good year (his batting eye was so sharp that he would swing and hit a speck of chewing gum for practice before every time he came to the plate—and never miss), the Padres in the June 11 game tried a Ted Williams shift against him, but it failed. The Cub hit a run-scoring double on the way to a 7–1 Chicago romp.

In the June 18 road-trip closer, Jenkins showed his form of the last three seasons, when he was the only major leaguer to win 20 in each. He shut out San Francisco, 6–0, to go over .500 for the first time in the year, with a win-loss record of 8-7.

Chicago had Cub Fever again, and when the team returned home, 39,895 came to the Friday, June 19 game that the St. Louis Cardinals won 5–3 in seventeen amazing innings. Both teams emptied their bullpens (one of the Cardinals' pitchers was Abernathy), Ken Holtzman got into the game as a pinch-hitter and Steve Barber took the loss for the Cubs by giving up two runs in the seventeenth after snuffing out a Cardinal rally the inning before.

When the Marquee network carrying Cub games and Cubs-related content debuted in February 2020, it showed a highlight from this game of the Cardinals' Dick Allen swinging at a Joe Decker pitch in the first inning.

A six-run first inning on June 20 resulted in an easy 8–3 Cub victory over the Cardinals. The Cubs started pulling away, in first place by four and a half games over the second-place Mets and by five over the third-place Pirates. The Cubs scored seemingly at will, and their pitching was superb.

And then, inexplicably and unexpectedly, came a June swoon of September 1969–like proportions.

It started out almost imperceptibly, as slumps inevitably do. On the first official day of summer, June 21, the Cubs banged out plenty of hits but had trouble driving runners in, and they lost a doubleheader to the Cardinals, 3–0 and 3–2.

Next came a *five-game* Wrigley Field series against the second-place New York Mets. The Cubs felt confident, holding a three-and-a-half-game lead and having won three of the five games between the two teams that season. But so did the Mets, who had won seven of their last ten games.

The Cubs had no problem scoring in the June 22 game, pushing five runs across the plate—but the Mets scored nine for the win.

The next day, June 23, the Cubs scored ten runs—and the Mets scored twelve. The Cubs' best pitcher of the day was rookie Jim Dunegan, who pitched three scoreless innings and left the game with a 10–8 lead. Closer Regan blew the lead and the game, giving up two runs in the ninth and another two in the tenth for his fourth loss of the year and his fifth blown save, putting his ERA at 4.18 and making Cub fans pine for Abernathy.

At this point, Regan, a veteran at age thirty-three, had pitched in half of the Cubs' games and "had appeared in a whopping 144 games" the previous two seasons, wrote Claerbaut. "Regan was burned out by being overused during the previous two seasons."[47]

National League umpires in 1970 behaved a lot more aggressively than they had a year before in trying to detect Regan's spitball, checking him out on the mound, making him take off his cap, looking at his glove and generally upsetting his rhythm. The combination of burnout and umpire vigilance made Regan much less effective.

The next day, the Cubs' management revealed that they had already made the decision to send Dunegan down to triple-A Tacoma. Had Regan held the Mets in check and the Cubs won, the victory would have created the unique situation of the winning pitcher, Dunegan, almost immediately being cut from the team. Ironically, of the Cubs' five pitchers that day, Barber was the only other pitcher besides Dunegan to hold the Mets scoreless, and that was Barber's last game for the team as well. He was released the next day. Barber would remain in the majors until 1974 after catching on with Atlanta for the remainder of 1970, pitching also for the California Angels and San Francisco Giants. Dunegan would never return to the majors.

The Cubs also acquired right-handed reliever Roberto Rodriguez, who already had pitched for the Oakland Athletics and San Diego Padres that year, in a three-team deal that sent Don Young, then in the minors but the Cubs' regular center fielder in 1969, to Oakland. Both Durocher and Santo had blasted Young's outfield misplays in a game against the Mets on July 8, 1969, a situation that experts considered a turning point helping lead to the eventual Cub collapse that year. Young's departure closed a chapter on 1969.

As Regan continued to falter, Durocher tried Rodriguez as the closer.

The media had been critical of Durocher for the collapse of 1969, but relations had taken a turn for the better, as the Cubs played well for the first two and a half months of 1970.

That week in June, however, their relationship completely soured when members of the media justifiably started complaining that Durocher withheld information from them just so he could reveal it on his five-nights-per-week radio show on WIND-AM and speculated that he was losing his sharpness and acumen. His managerial style, learned in the 1920s, was to attempt to goad, harass and insult players into performing better. That style proved increasingly out of step with the 1970s. Durocher's harshest critic was the *Chicago Today*'s Rick Talley.

In a postgame June 23 interview, a baseball writer asked Durocher if he planned any lineup changes for the next day's doubleheader. Durocher said he did not know.

Only an hour later on his radio show, Durocher said he would bench Santo, hitting .235 with forty-five strikeouts, in the next day's doubleheader in favor of Popovich. Durocher had not bothered to tell Santo, who learned of the benching while listening to the radio. The manager also revealed that he had decided to bench Banks against right-handed pitchers and that he planned on playing Hickman at first and James in center for most games, disclosed the pending Dunegan demotion and hinted at the upcoming Barber release.

Durocher, who in earlier decades was considered a "players' manager" (he even had been a playing manager from 1939 to 1945), at age sixty-five had become increasingly distant from the players, often not telling them information they needed to know, revealing it instead on the radio and generally creating tension with the team. Callison said of his strained relations with Durocher, "It got to the point where I even was worried how I looked in batting practice."[48]

Durocher had also been irritated with the media, because he had been "accused by writers and broadcasters of idling Banks out of envy."[49] Yet Durocher himself admitted in the *Sun-Times* that he had tried to sit Banks down since 1966. "How many times did I try to retire him in '66? How many first basemen did I try that year? He'd sit there on the bench…and finally I'd say, 'OK, go on out there and play.'"[50]

Manager Leo Durocher's controversial WIND-AM radio show caused disruption on the team in late June, forcing him to give up his broadcasting job. *National Baseball Hall of Fame Library.*

In the next day's doubleheader, with Popovich at third for both games, Banks and Santo on the bench, Rodriguez in the bullpen and Dunegan heading to Tacoma, the Cubs lost both June 24 contests and dropped into second place. The *Sun-Times* headline screamed, "1969 Replay? Help, Help! Cubs No. 2 after Met 9–5, 6–1 Sweep."[51] With Santo and Banks back in the lineup, the Cubs then lost the home stand's June 25 finale, 8–3, with Rodriguez pitching

The midseason acquisition of Milt Pappas gave the Cubs the fourth starting pitcher they needed to settle their rotation. *National Baseball Hall of Fame Library.*

three and two-thirds scoreless innings and the Cubs suffering the indignity of Met third-baseman Joe Foy stealing home—one of ten Met stolen bases in the series in eleven tries.

Five straight losses to the Mets. Seven straight losses overall. After more than two months leading the Eastern Division, the Cubs were no longer in first place.

Immediately after the game, Cub management announced two more moves. One was another that had been telegraphed by Durocher on the radio—the return of Al Spangler, one of the heroes of '69, from triple-A Tacoma.

The other surprised everyone; the Cubs had acquired another player with a bad reputation, right-handed pitcher Milt Pappas. At urging of the Cubs' traveling secretary, Blake Cullen, who knew Pappas from Cullen's days working for the Atlanta Braves, the team bought Pappas from the Braves for $50,000. The Society for American Baseball Research's Warren Corbett wrote that Pappas "acknowledged his reputation as a clubhouse lawyer—a troublemaker....A man of a thousand grievances, he alienated many teammates as well as management."[52]

Jim Bouton wrote in *Ball Four* that early the previous year, the Cubs had passed on acquiring Bouton because he also had a reputation as a clubhouse lawyer.[53] Had they acquired him, the iconic *Ball Four* would have been about the 1969 Cubs.

Also part of Pappas's bad-boy reputation was his readiness to throw at opposing batters. Billy Williams later said that Cubs' players never were concerned about pitchers throwing "chin music" at the Cubs if Pappas was on the mound. "If they did, he would go after them and knock their players down," Williams noted. "Whenever he pitched, you didn't worry about a guy coming close."[54]

Pappas was a stellar acquisition for the Cubs, moving into the starting rotation and winning ten games in 1970. He would win seventeen for the Cubs in each of the next two seasons, leading the league in shutouts in 1971 and pitching a no-hitter that nearly was a perfect game in 1972.

HANK AGUIRRE

The Cubs hastened the departure of pitcher Hank Aguirre from the major leagues, and he eventually moved to Detroit to run a $100 million auto-parts manufacturing and supply company. *Chicago National League Ball Club Inc. (Chicago Cubs).*

The Cubs made room for Pappas's June 26 arrival with yet another inexplicable move, however, outright releasing left-handed reliever Hank Aguirre, whose won-loss record was a neat 3-0 at the time. The Cubs had already gotten rid of reliever Ted Abernathy, and Durocher was pinning his hopes on the untested Rodriguez coming out of the bullpen more as Regan was faltering. Releasing Aguirre from an increasingly erratic bullpen made no sense from a baseball standpoint. It made even less sense from a public-relations standpoint, as Aguirre, one of the heroes of 1969, was popular among fans, particularly Mexican American fans.

Some of the Bleacher Bums had traveled to Pittsburgh, and Aguirre after his release went looking for them for comfort. The Bums sang songs for him deep into the night.[55]

Had the Cubs kept Aguirre, it is not out of the question that he could have become the closer despite being a lefty. In 1989, the Cubs would use lefthander Mitch Williams as their closer in a league-leading seventy-six games and ended up winning the division.

Aguirre was the kind of straight-arrow that conservative Cub management generally loved. He certainly had not worn out his welcome with the team, who hired him back as a coach and public relations liaison in 1972.

After leaving baseball, Aguirre mortgaged his home to begin a Detroit auto-parts manufacturing and supply company called Mexican Industries, which became a $100 million enterprise, employing more than one thousand people—more than 85 percent of them minorities. He also became a community activist. "In Mexican Village—Detroit's version of East L.A.— Aguirre became a god," according to the *Los Angeles Times.*[56]

Santo had always found Spangler's hitting and fielding tips helpful, so he was pleased at the outfielder's return.

On to Pittsburgh for the last three games ever played at Forbes Field, as the Pirates would open their next home stand on July 16 at brand-new Three Rivers Stadium. The Cubs also had been the Pirates' opponents when Forbes opened on June 30, 1909, with the Cubs winning, 3–2. This time, the Cubs would lose all three. Their eighth loss in a row, 2–1 on June 27, dropped them into third place, with the Mets in first and the Pirates in second. The next day, they lost a twin bill, 3–2 and 4–1, in front of 40,918 for the last games at Forbes (a crowd larger than any at the stadium in the previous fourteen years, including the 1960 World Series). Pappas took the loss in the nightcap in his first Cub appearance, bringing the streak to ten in a row.

On to St. Louis to lose two more. In an effort to shake things up, Durocher started Santo in left field on June 29. Williams's consecutive-game streak of 1,053 remained intact as he entered the game in the ninth inning of the 8–6 loss, which put the Cubs one game under .500 at 35-36. The Cubs sold reserve outfielder Jimmie Hall to the Atlanta Braves that day.

The next night, June 30, they lost, 5–4; Durocher fined starting pitcher Decker for leaving the mound before Rodriguez arrived. Sportswriter Talley believed it was "an incident that Durocher obviously created to use the rookie pitcher as a scapegoat to detract from the 12-game losing streak."[57]

Earlier that day, doubtlessly at the behest of owner Wrigley and vice-president Holland, WIND-AM Radio sent Durocher a telegram saying that his services were no longer needed on the airwaves, and Wrigley told the media that Durocher would remain the manager of the Cubs.

Closer Phil Regan's off year was one of the reasons manager Leo Durocher found his bullpen to be unreliable. *National Baseball Hall of Fame Library.*

The not-always-truthful Durocher said, "I want it made clear this is my own decision."[58] Durocher had signed a $40,000 contract with WIND—an impressive salary in 1970—and it is doubtful that he wanted to give it up despite the turmoil his radio show caused.

So the Cubs had lost twelve in a row, with an overall record of 10-18 for a dismal .357 percentage for the month. The team had a chance to win most of those games, as eight of the losses had been by three runs or less. Twelve consecutive losses tied the Cubs' all-time mark set in 1944. The team was in first place when the streak started; after the June 30 game, they were under .500 at 35-37, in fourth place behind the Mets, Pirates and Cardinals.

No one factor caused the 1970 streak. When the Cubs hit well, their hurlers pitched poorly. When the pitching was good, the Cubs quit hitting. Hickman still was hitting .327, but everyone else was under .300, with Santo at .224 and Banks on the bench. With Santo having such a poor season, he often heard boos at Wrigley Field. Among pitchers, Holtzman was 8-5, Hands was 9-7, Jenkins was back under .500 at 8-9 and Decker was 1-4 and in Durocher's doghouse. Pappas looked to take his spot in the rotation. Regan had six blown saves, five losses and a 4.44 ERA, and Durocher increasingly called on Colborn, Gura and Rodriguez out of the bullpen.

Durocher, who had kicked business agents out of the clubhouse because they caused a distraction, had himself become a distraction because of his radio-show antics.

It was "some kind of month," to use Durocher's parlance.

8

JULY

SIZZLING HOT

In July, Casey Kasem's American Top 40 debuted on the radio. Explorer Thor Heyerdahl crossed the Atlantic Ocean on a raft. The Aswan Dam opened in Egypt. News anchor Chet Huntley retired from NBC-TV. The Cincinnati Reds' Johnny Bench hit three consecutive home runs off of Philadelphia Phillies pitcher Steve Carlton. And the Cubs started the month in third place, three and a half games behind.

The Cubs finally broke the streak in the last game of the road trip on July 1, as Jenkins tossed a complete game, four-hit shutout.

Back at Wrigley as the holiday weekend began on Friday, July 3, a loss against the Pirates saw the highest total of runs scored against the Cubs all season: sixteen. Yet the Cubs had nearly won the game, having been on top 13–10 going into the eighth inning. But Gura, Rodriguez and Regan all failed to hold the lead, with no Ab and Ag available to save the day. Spangler paid an immediate dividend by slugging a pinch-hit double in the bottom of the ninth and scoring, but the rally fell short. The next day's *Sun-Times'* headline read, "Cub Pitching Torn to Pieces 16–14."[59]

The traditional Fourth of July doubleheader saw the Cubs lose the opener to the Pirates, 10–6, but Pappas paid his first dividend as he beat Pittsburgh, 7–2, in the nightcap, tossing eight and one-third solid innings, with Gura getting the save.

Milt Pappas paid his first dividend for the Cubs when he beat Pittsburgh, 7–2, on July 4. *Chicago History Museum, ICHi-076834; Bob Langer for* Chicago Daily News, *photographer.*

In the 5–2 loss of July 5, Cub baserunner Popovich, Pirate first baseman Al Oliver and first-base umpire Tom Gorman all collided into one another, with Gorman suffering a broken right ankle. Lying on the ground, Gorman made no call, and Durocher came out of the dugout to ask, "Is Popovich safe or out?" Gorman, stunned from the collision, said, "Who's asking?" "It's Leo," Durocher replied. "He's out!" Gorman concluded.

Gorman was not the only one in a foul mood, with Cub pitcher Colborn and Pirate pitcher Dock Ellis both throwing beanballs. While Durocher talked things over to plate umpire Nick Colosi, Ellis yelled a comment at Durocher, who moved toward Ellis. Both dugouts emptied, and a brawl ensued, with Reynolds leading the Cub charge and ending up with face and leg injuries and a torn shirt. The brawl sent Pirate manager Danny Murtaugh to the hospital. Although umpires did not exactly love Durocher, Colosi put the blame on Ellis, not Durocher.

In a subsequent five-game Wrigley Field series against Montreal, the Cubs fared much better than they had in their 0-5 series against the Mets, with the Cubs winning four out of five from the Expos.

Rodriguez, now the closer, earned the save in the first game of the July 6 doubleheader, a 3–2 Cub victory with Santo banging out a two-run homer. It was the third baseman's day; Santo starred in the nightcap with eight RBI, four coming on a grand slam, and starting pitcher Decker earned what would be his last victory of the year in a 14–2 laugher. Santo called it "the game of my life."[60] After another Cub win on July 7, with Rodriguez earning his first victory of the year in a 10–7 slugfest, the Cubs split a July 8 doubleheader, with Pappas tallying his first complete-game win for Chicago. The Cubs had climbed back to .500.

Less than two weeks after releasing left-handed reliever Aguirre, on July 9, the Cubs endeavored to replace him by trading right-handed pitcher Reynolds, the hero of the brawl only four days before, to the California Angels for aging left-handed reliever Juan Pizarro. Why not just keep Aguirre, particularly since acquiring Pizarro cost the Cubs a player? Or why not rely on a young lefty like Gura? Reynolds said of Durocher, "He'd rather go with a 40-year-old veteran than a kid with potential."[61]

Ron Santo had what he called "the game of my life" against the Montreal Expos on July 6, when he knocked in eight runs in the nightcap of a doubleheader. *National Baseball Hall of Fame Library.*

Pizarro generally proved ineffective for the Cubs in 1970, with no wins and one save in twelve games. He did pay off in 1971, when he moved into the Cubs' starting rotation.

While Aguirre manifested the type of solid citizen behavior Cub management usually loved, Pizarro, on the other hand, exhibited a "great love of eating, drinking, gambling, and carousing," according to Rory Costello of the Society for American Baseball Research, and he had earned a bad-dude reputation as a young Milwaukee Brave when he threw some chin music to the beloved Stan Musial.[62]

At least the Cubs' management once again showed a willingness to trade for a carouser if they thought he could help the team.

The Cubs also reactivated the finally healed Hundley that day. Had the catcher not been injured for most of the first half of the season, one can assume the Cubs

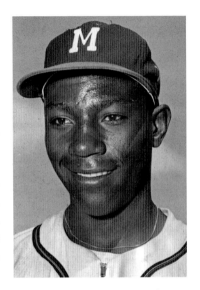

The Cubs made another surprising acquisition in July by bringing on pitcher Juan Pizarro, who had earned a bad-dude reputation as a young Milwaukee Brave by throwing at Stan Musial. *National Baseball Hall of Fame Library.*

would have been better, possibly much better, than their 42-42 record. Jenkins, who much preferred being caught by Hundley than any other backstop, would likely have had a better record than the 9-10 he had posted up to that time. With Hundley's superb abilities with young pitchers and Durocher relying on hurlers Colborn, Dunegan, Gura and Reynolds more than anyone would have expected (Durocher did not like pitching the rookies, but Regan's off year had forced the manager to use them more), under Hundley's tutelage the youngsters likely would have been posting breakout rookie seasons.

The last three games before the All-Star break saw the Cubs win two of three from the Phillies to go back over .500 at 43-42. The July 10 game, in which Jenkins gave up only five hits (two from Gamble) and won, 2–0, took only one hour and forty-eight minutes. In the 10–4 Cub loss of July 11, Gamble tallied another two hits, Selma pitched scoreless ball for the Phils and Pizarro, in his first Cub appearance, gave up four runs. After the Cubs won the last game before the All-Star break, 10–2, the *Sun-Times* headline read, "Cubs on Upbeat." They were in third place behind the first-place Pirates and second-place Mets.[63]

For the first time since 1957, fans in 1970 elected the starting lineups for the All-Star Game, and they chose two Cubs to start: Kessinger and Beckert. National League manager Gil Hodges of the Mets, responsible for picking the backups and coaches, added Hickman and his .335 average and Durocher as third-base coach. Hodges left Williams, now hitting .312 with twenty-six home runs and eighty RBI, to watch the game at home.

Tuesday, July 14, saw the All-Star Game played at brand-new Riverfront Stadium in Cincinnati. President Richard Nixon threw out the first pitch in front of a sellout crowd of 51,838 at only the second All-Star Game broadcast in prime time.

Kessinger went two-for-two at the plate, and Beckert made a nice tag on the Milwaukee Brewers' Tommy Harper, who tried to steal second. But the Cub star of the evening was Hickman, who almost didn't make it to the game. Hickman's original fight had been canceled, and he was forced to take a later one, not actually arriving in Cincinnati until near the end of batting practice.

The replay of Cincinnati's Pete Rose barreling into Cleveland catcher Ray Fosse in the bottom of the twelfth inning to win the game for the National League, 5–4, has been shown on television thousands of times, but seldom is it mentioned that it was Hickman who got the single to drive in Rose, who had been on second and was waved home by third-base coach Durocher.

When league play resumed on July 16, the Cubs hit a win-some, lose-some stretch in which they remained in third place, five games behind Pittsburgh. They split a four-game series in the Astrodome. The 7–3 win of July 18 saw young Colborn earn his fourth save and the oddity of Hickman coming in to play center field in the seventh inning to spell starter James. In the July 19 Cub win, Pappas pitched another complete game and the Cubs won, 7–1. Then the team moved on to Atlanta, where the Cubs lost two of three.

The Cubs came home on July 22 to face the Reds, who were running away with the National League West with a .702 percentage and an eleven-game lead. Banks went on the disabled list because of knee problems, and the *Sun-Times* speculated as to whether he would ever return.[64] While injured, Mr. Cub also joined the WGN-TV broadcast team.

Always unpredictable, the Cubs swept the two-game series, routing the Big Red Machine in the opener, 10–2.

Almost one hundred games into the season, the Reds had yet to suffer a shutout—until they ran into Pappas on July 23. He beat them with a complete game 1–0 gem, the best game Pappas had pitched in years, against the team with the best record in baseball.

The sweep showed that the Cubs could beat the Big Red Machine both with hitting and pitching, giving the team confidence that it could win against Cincinnati in the National League Championship Series—if only the Cubs could get there.

The Atlanta Braves then came to Chicago for a four-game series, with the Cubs winning the July 24 opener, 11–1, and suddenly finding themselves on a four-game winning streak. Atlanta won the next two, though, with the Cubs taking the last game of the series.

An off day on July 27 saw Cub radio broadcaster Lou Boudreau inducted into the National Baseball Hall of Fame in Cooperstown, New York. Boudreau was a star and manager for the Cleveland Indians in the 1940s, and he also later managed the Cubs.

The Astros came to Wrigley Field next, and the Cubs won two out of three. In the 9–2 July 29 win, the usually slow-footed Cubs stole six bases.

The Cubs made the biggest, best and most surprising deal of the year when, on that day, they purchased Joe Pepitone from the Astros. The Cubs also later sent infielder Roger Metzger to the Astros as part of the deal.

For a team that in the past had always been willing to pass on partiers and trade for solid citizens, the Pepitone acquisition was truly amazing. If Ernie Banks were Mr. Cub, Pepitone was the Anti-Cub.

Trouble had surrounded Pepitone since his teenage years, when a high-school classmate shot him with a gun. With the New York Yankees, he was at the center of brawls against the Detroit Tigers and Cleveland Indians.[65] In his 1975 book *Joe, You Coulda Made Us Proud*, Pepitone admitted that during his career he was a drinker, a marijuana smoker, got in bar fights and was a playboy.[66]

Despite being a native New Yorker popular with the city's Italian American community, an All-Star and a three-time Gold Glove winner who had twice received votes for American League Most Valuable Player, Pepitone, after eight years, was shipped by conservative Yankee management to Houston.

Pepitone at first welcomed the move from the American League to the National. At the time, NL pitchers tended to throw fastballs and sliders, while in the AL, pitchers tended to throw breaking balls and changeups. Pepitone was a fastball hitter.

However, it took Pepitone only a half season to wear out his welcome in even more conservative Houston. Astros manager Harry Walker and Pepitone did not get along, but Pepitone and Durocher, who had been a roistering player himself, got along just fine. In fact, Pepitone said of Durocher, "He was an older version of me."[67]

Left: Longtime Cub radio broadcaster Lou Boudreau (*left*) entered the National Baseball Hall of Fame in July. He was congratulated by Commissioner Bowie Kuhn. *National Baseball Hall of Fame Library.*

Right: Although controversy followed Joe Pepitone throughout his career, it skipped Chicago in 1970 as the free spirit immediately became a fan favorite and helped the Cubs back into contention. *National Baseball Hall of Fame Library.*

Acquiring Pepitone was just about the last move anyone expected from conservative Cub management. Like the Barber, Pappas and Pizarro acquisitions, it showed their seriousness about winning in 1970—even if that meant acquiring "bad boys" who did not fit the Cubs' persona.

With a magnanimity they rarely exhibited, Cub management was willing to overlook Pepitone's personal foibles and hoped that his postseason experience, skill at the plate and tested hand at both first base and center field would give the Cubs a shot in the arm.

And they were right.

Surprisingly, the media at first did not celebrate this extreme departure from hidebound conservative Cub tradition. The *Sun-Times* headline of July 30 was a bit snarky: "'Hair' at Wrigley: Pepitone a Cub," referring to Pepitone's long hair and bushy sideburns, unusual among ballplayers at the time.[68] A caption under a picture of Pepitone in the August 2 *Sun-Times* made fun of Pepitone: "He looks (choose one) happy, unhappy, confused, sleepy, bored, indifferent, angry, wishful, ready to belt the photographer."[69]

Bill Hands ended July as the Cubs' best starting pitcher with a record of thirteen wins and eight losses. The Cub bullpen was located down the left-field line in that era. *ST-19060048-0001*, Chicago Sun-Times *collection, Chicago History Museum.*

The players and fans felt differently. Pepitone joined the Cubs at Cincinnati for a July 31 doubleheader, and he was pleasantly surprised at the other players' enthusiasm about him joining the team. Out on the field, he was perplexed by all the cheering for him—until Santo told him the Bleacher Bums were there from Chicago. The Bums even wrote a song called "Around the League with Pepitone" and sang it to him at the hotel that night.[70]

In the doubleheader, the Cubs' first-ever games at Riverfront Stadium, Pepitone started both games in center field, banging out two hits in game one, singling in the winning run and adding another hit and RBI in the nightcap. The Cubs swept the twin bill. The *Sun-Times* headline of August 1 called them the "Charging Cubs."[71]

They finished the month still in third place at 52-49 but only three games out of first. Their record in July was a good one: 19-12, a .613 percentage. Williams's and Hickman's batting averages remained over .300, Santo had gotten his up to .253 and Pepitone, also hitting .253, had taken over for the fancy-fielding but light-hitting Cleo James. Hickman was now the regular first baseman. Durocher started platooning Callison in right field and pinch-hitting for him, a situation that startled Callison, as it had never happened in Philadelphia. Hands's win-loss record was 13-8, Holtzman's was 11-9, Jenkins's was 12-12, Pappas was firmly in the rotation and Rodriguez was the closer.

With the acquisitions of Pappas, Pepitone and Rodriguez, Cub management showed that it still believed the team could win, and those players had come through. Now, it was up to the rest of the Cubs to deliver.

9

AUGUST

SUDDENLY, THIS SUMMER

In August, government officials let Black Panther leader Huey Newton out of jail. Christine Perfect joined the band Fleetwood Mac. Former St. Louis Cardinal Curt Flood lost his antitrust suit against Major League Baseball. The Pittsburgh Pirates' Roberto Clemente had two straight five-hit games. Singer Elton John performed in the United States for the first time. And the Cubs started the month in third place, three games behind.

Still on the road trip, the Cubs lost their first two games of August to Cincinnati. In the August 1 game with the Cubs in the lead after seven innings, starter Pappas told pitching coach Joe Becker he was tired. Spangler pinch-hit for Pappas in the top of the eighth, but in the bottom of the frame, Regan and Gura gave up four runs, and the Cubs ended up losing, 6–4. Pappas came to the Cubs as a pitcher with a reputation for not finishing games. From then on, Durocher expected him to go nine innings.

The Cubs did not let the losses bother them; on August 3 in New York, Jenkins three-hit the Mets, 6–1. It was a game in which New York fans greeted their prodigal son Pepitone with a chorus of boos. The Cubs lost the second game of the series and then moved on to Montreal to take two of three. In the August 5 contest, Durocher reaffirmed his increasing willingness to rely on young pitchers. Gura started and pitched a complete-game, 11–3 win. The next night, Durocher dropped Santo to seventh in the order against the Expos. Santo, formerly Durocher's biggest booster, blasted him to the media and then went four-for-four with a home run. Holtzman gave up no hits in the first seven innings as the Cubs won, 4–2.

Coach Joey Amalfitano attempted to mediate the dispute between Santo and Durocher, to no avail. Durocher was becoming more angry, defensive and withdrawn.

Philadelphia was the last stop on the road trip, with the Cubs losing three of four.

With pitching coach Becker suffering from ill health due to a heart condition, Durocher brought in one of his old buddies from his New York Giant days, Herman Franks, to replace Becker. Not content to merely make a necessary move, Durocher needled the team by telling the media he expected Franks to "light a fire under those guys." Jenkins did note that Franks's tutelage "gave us a lift for a while."[72] Franks later managed the Cubs to a surprising resurgence in 1977.

On his return from the road trip, new Cub Pepitone was surprised when a chauffeured limousine met him. A driver who called himself Fabulous Howard had decided to squire Pepitone around town in the limo for the rest of the season for free, announcing Pepitone's arrival at various places by playing the "River Kwai March" on the Cadillac's horn and literally rolling out a red carpet when Pepitone exited the limo to enter the Executive House Hotel, where Pepitone stayed. Howard figured the publicity that was sure to come would help him build his chauffeur business.

As the season progressed, Pepitone became one of the most popular sports figures in the city. The *Chicago Tribune* wrote that Pepitone's "growing popularity would be a threat to Mayor [Richard J.] Daley if he ever decides to enter Chicago politics."[73]

"Chicago was the best thing that ever happened to me," Pepitone wrote.[74]

The home stand saw the West Coast teams swing into Wrigley for ten days for the last time in the season. The Cubs did well, and Pepitone received a standing ovation his first time at bat. He also found the iconic ivy a good place to hide drugs during the game.[75]

A midseason coaching change seldom makes a difference in a team's fortunes, but coach Herman Franks joining the Cubs gave the team "a lift for a while," according to Ferguson Jenkins. *National Baseball Hall of Fame Library*.

The Cubs took two of three from the Giants, with Jenkins and Pappas both tossing complete-game victories. Pappas homered off Gaylord Perry in the 6–3 win of August 13.

Next came the Dodgers, who split their four games with the Cubs. In a 13–9 August 14 loss, Billy Grabarkewitz of the Dodgers had a career day, with eleven total bases, and Cub relievers Gura, Rodriguez, Pizarro and Decker pitched poorly in front of 40,591 fans.

That prompted the *Sun-Times'* Edgar Munzel to run an interview with Baltimore scout Frank Lane, one of the top executives in baseball history, in an August 17 article titled, "Trading Abby was Cubs' Big Goof."[76] In the article, Lane said that trading Abernathy was the Cubs' "biggest mistake" of the season. Abernathy was 6–3 with a 1.95 ERA for Kansas City at the time. "The Cubs don't have anybody out there who is capable of doing that kind of a job," Lane concluded.

The Cubs finished off the home stand by taking two of three from the Padres. Despite Pepitone's popularity with the fans and his getting two hits and an RBI in the Cubs' 7–0 victory of August 17, the *Sun-Times* inexplicably continued to make fun of him, calling him a "pretty boy" in a photo caption.[77]

Nonetheless, Pepitone had a good effect on the team, not only with his hitting and fielding, but also with his sense of humor in the clubhouse. "He keeps the guys laughing and relaxed," Kessinger said.[78] Beckert, and also the witty coach Rube Walker, now had another competitor in the team jokester department.

The team, in turn, had a good effect on Pepitone, who cut way back on his partying to concentrate on baseball.

In the series finale on August 19, the Cubs won easily, 12–2, cranking out seven home runs, including career-high number thirty-five for Williams.

Despite the 6–4 home stand, the Cubs' strong hitting and the large crowds indicating the fans' continuing belief in the team, they still languished in third place, four games behind Pittsburgh, as they headed for the traditionally tough West Coast.

With Banks healthy enough to come off the disabled list, the Cubs decided to send pitcher Decker to the minors to make room for the first baseman, officially ending the team's five-month experiment with slotting the rookie in the pitching rotation.

Lorrie Ross, Decker's sister, gave a surprising reason why her brother often found himself in Durocher's doghouse, saying that Decker and the manager "had some issues because my brother was really good looking. Leo Durocher considered himself the ladies' man. So I think they had a little bit of conflict about that."[79]

Left: Pitcher Joe Decker often found himself in manager Leo Durocher's doghouse for a surprising reason: Durocher allegedly thought Decker was too handsome. *Chicago National League Ball Club Inc. (Chicago Cubs).*

Right: John Callison, whose first year with the Cubs was 1970, said he loved playing for Chicago but not for manager Leo Durocher. *Chicago National League Ball Club Inc. (Chicago Cubs).*

The rest of the way, Banks would often start at first, with Hickman in right and Callison sitting down. Decker would return to the team in September. Callison loved playing with the Cubs but could not stand Durocher, who Callison felt almost drove him out of baseball.[80] Callison found sitting on the bench "torture."[81]

The trip started with the Cubs dropping two of three in San Francisco, but the August 22 game was a 15–0 Cub rout, in which Holtzman again took a no-hitter into the eighth inning before the Giants' Hal Lanier became the villain by lining a single to left field with one out. Game three of the series was a heartbreaker, as the Cubs had it won, leading 3–2 in the ninth inning. First, an error by Santo, and then another error by Kessinger that would have been the third and final San Francisco out, resulted in a 4–3 Giant victory.

Yet the Cubs did not let the blown game bother them, and they immediately beat the Dodgers in Los Angeles the next night. They lost the next two, however, and at the end of the Dodger series, the Cubs remained in third place, four and a half games out.

A Bill Hands shutout against the San Diego Padres on August 30 put the Cubs only one game out of first place. *Jewel-Osco.*

Then suddenly came three games in San Diego that *Chicago Today* described as "weird, wonderful."[82]

In game one of the series on August 27, Pappas again went the distance to beat the Padres, 5–1. The Pirates did not play that day, so the Cubs gained half a game. In game two on August 28, Jenkins went the distance, beating the Padres, 8–4. It was the first time since June 3 that the Cubs had come from behind to win in the eighth or ninth inning.[83] The Pirates lost to the Giants, 5–1, putting the Cubs only three games behind. The next day, the Cubs did not play while the Pirates lost a 10–9 heartbreaker to the Giants, while the Mets lost a similar 9–8 heartbreaker to the Astros. That moved the Cubs up to two and a half games out, tied for second place with New York.

On Sunday, August 30, Bill Hands of the Cubs and Dave Roberts of the Padres went into the ninth inning with each having pitched eight innings of scoreless baseball. In the top of the ninth, after Roberts walked Hickman and Santo, Pepitone blasted a home run deep into the right-field stands. Hands held the Padres scoreless in the bottom of the ninth.

"Cubs Game Out! Pepitone Homer Rips Padres 3–0," and "Cubs Leap into 2d; A Game Out of 1st," read the *Sun-Times* headlines the next day.[84] The Pirates had lost a doubleheader to the Giants for six losses in a row, and the Mets had again lost to Houston, moving the Cubs up to one game behind, in sole possession of second place.

Suddenly, a pennant race!

10

SEPTEMBER

FINISHING THE SONG OFF-KEY

In September, Elvis Presley began his first concert tour since 1958. Rock star Jimi Hendrix passed away. Marxist Salvador Allende won the presidency in Chile. The Chicago White Sox used a record forty-one players in a doubleheader and lost both games. Baseball commissioner Bowie Kuhn suspended Detroit Tigers pitcher Denny McLain for carrying a firearm. And the Cubs started the month in second place, one game behind.

The September 1 game was one of those pressure-packed pennant-race contests. The fifth-place Phillies faced the Cubs at Wrigley, and with the Cubs looking good through seven innings with a 2–0 lead, the Phillies tied the game in the eighth. Selma held the Cubs scoreless in the ninth and tenth. Regan, recently back as the closer after Rodriguez had for some inexplicable reason fallen out of favor with Durocher, worked out of a jam left to him by Holtzman in the ninth inning—but he ended up losing the game, 3–2, in thirteen innings.

So the Cubs still needed a closer. Immediately, they purchased veteran Bob Miller from the White Sox—a great move, but another that Cub management would eventually bungle. Miller would save two key games in the September 1970 stretch and make the team again in 1971. After Miller pitched in only two games for the Cubs that year, they gave him his unconditional release on May 10. Pitching the rest of 1971 for the Padres and Pirates, Miller would become one of the top relievers in the National League with eight wins, ten saves and a microscopic 1.64 ERA. He would continue to pitch in the majors through 1974.

Billy Williams set what was then the National League record for consecutive games when he finished his streak at 1,117. *National Baseball Hall of Fame Library.*

Outfielder-catcher Adrian Garrett, who had won the Texas League's home run title with twenty-nine for San Antonio, and young outfielder Brock Davis, also were called up to the big club.

The Cubs bounced right back on September 2, when they scored their highest single-game run total of the season, winning 17–2, with midseason acquisitions Pepitone and Pappas both hitting home runs and Miller finishing the game on the mound. Gamble reminded the Cubs what they had lost by trading him when he hit a home run to left-center in the ninth inning.

In the final game of the series, Cub fans experienced something they had not seen since 1963: Billy Williams did not play. After 1,117 consecutive games played, at the time a National League record (since eclipsed by Steve Garvey), Williams asked Durocher for a day off. The Cubs won, 7–2, and sat a half game out of first, only .004 percentage points behind the Pirates.

The Mets came into town next, and mid- and late-season acquisitions Rodriguez, Pizarro and Miller pitched effectively, with Rodriguez tallying a win and Miller earning the save in a 7–4 victory in front of 39,981 fans on September 4. The game featured the oddity of starting pitcher Hands, one of the weakest batters in the league, actually slugging his way out of the ballgame. After Hands hit a rare double in the sixth inning, Durocher removed him in favor of a pinch-runner. For once, the "play it safe" manager relied on his bullpen to win the game, and the gamble paid off. The Cubs remained a half game out, only .003 percentage points behind.

Yet, on September 5, the Cubs suffered a big setback, losing to the Mets and Jerry Koosman, 5–3, while the Pirates beat the Phillies twice to open a game-and-a-half lead over the Cubs. The Cubs had unlocked the Wrigley Field gates an hour early to accommodate huge numbers of people clamoring to get in; the crowd numbered 37,821 and put the Cubs over the million-and-a-half mark in attendance.

A Cub rainout and a Pittsburgh win on September 6 put the Pirate lead at two games.

Labor Day saw the Cubs make their debut in Pittsburgh's brand-new Three Rivers Stadium with a doubleheader split against the Pirates. The Cubs remained two games back but now in third place as the Mets were one and a half behind. A 10–3 Cub laugher against the Pirates the next day, the Cubs' eighth win in their last eleven games, put Chicago back to only one game behind.

Back home against the Expos on September 9, the Cubs were tied going into the ninth when, in the top half of the frame, Montreal's Bobby Wine singled in ex-Cub Adolfo Phillips, and the Cubs lost another heartbreaker, 3–2, with Rodriguez taking the loss after succeeding Miller on the mound. But the Cubs bounced back the next day with a 9–3 win. Banks starred in the game with a home run and four RBI, and Pizarro earned the save. Durocher clearly was relying on the midseason acquisitions in the bullpen. The Mets had tied the Pirates for first, and the Cubs were a game behind both. A Met loss to the Cardinals the next night when the Cubs and Pirates did not play put the Pirates back in first alone, with the Mets a half game back and the Cubs one behind.

The Cubs lost a heartbreaker to the Montreal Expos, 3–2, on September 9 during the stretch run. *National Baseball Hall of Fame Library*.

The Pirates came to Chicago as the Cubs' next Wrigley Field opponents. In front of 33,199, the Cubs entered the ninth inning down only 2–1, but Pizarro gave up two runs on a Willie Stargell homer, and Miller gave up one more run. Hickman hit a three-run homer in the bottom of the ninth that would have won the game had the Cub pitchers held the Pirates in the top of the frame. The Cubs were now two games back, in third place, with the Mets only one-half game behind in second.

September 13 saw a pivotal matchup between the Pirates and the Cubs on a rainy Sunday. The Cubs looked lackluster the whole day, down 2–1 going into the ninth inning. Callison and Popovich hit easy grounders to second baseman Dave Cash for two quick outs. Willie Smith then batted for Cub pitcher Bill Hands and hit a routine pop fly to center fielder Matty Alou, who pounded his glove in the universal "I got this" symbol. Pirate pitcher Steve Blass, "certain he had just completed a five-hit victory, jumped up and down on the mound in glee."[85]

And then, in the cold, wet wind, Alou dropped the fly ball. Smith ended up on second base.

Ken Rudolph ran for Smith. Kessinger, the next batter, scooted a groundball single between first and second base, and Rudolph scored the tying run. Beckert then singled, moving Kessinger to second.

Blass had lost his composure. Pirate manager Danny Murtaugh brought in lefty pitcher George Brunet to face Williams. On a 1-0 count, Williams lined a single into left field, scoring Kessinger for a 3–2 victory.

A loss that would have dropped the Cubs to three games back instead turned into a win that put them only one game back, with the Mets second by half a game.

The *Sun-Times*' Jerome Holtzman wrote: "Afterwards in the clubhouse, Durocher was more jubilant than at any time this season. Durocher saw Joe Amalfitano, one of his coaches, reach for a pint of milk and said, 'No, no, Joey! Not today! Today we drink scotch.'"[86]

Bill Gleason of the *Sun-Times* wrote, "The Cubs won Sunday after three outs in the ninth."[87]

Writer Holtzman compared the possible impact of the game to that of the game in which Gabby Hartnett hit his "homer in the gloaming" in 1938 to propel the Cubs to the pennant. While the game certainly gave the Cubs a lift, the loss may have actually inspired the Pirates to play better the rest of the season. Several Pirates would go on to say that they wanted to win the division so Alou would not suffer for the rest of his life by people saying the Pirates lost the pennant because of his error.

Next came the Cardinals, and fate continued to smile on the Cubs, as another windblown misplay, this time by Cardinal right-fielder Luis Melendez in the sixth inning, helped the Cubs win, 5–3 on September 15. The game inspired Jerome Holtzman to write a poem in the *Sun-Times*: "Dear Matty Alou: / It isn't just you. / A rookie named Melendez / Just blew one, too."[88] With the newcomers in the bullpen recently ineffectual, Durocher went back to Regan for the save. The Cubs remained one game out, now in second place.

Unfortunately, the Cubs' hitting went to sleep for the next two games, as the Cardinals won, 8–1, on September 16 and 9–2 on September 17. Chicago dropped two games back in third place. Rookie call-up Roe Skidmore pinch-hit for Decker and got a hit. That was his only major-league at bat, making Skidmore only one of a handful of former major leaguers whose lifetime average is 1.000.

Wrigley and Holland, however, continued adding players to try to push the Cubs over the finish line. On September 16, during the Cardinal series, they purchased two-time National League batting champion Tommy Davis from the Oakland Athletics. Durocher said he would employ Davis primarily as a pinch-hitter and give him an occasional start in the outfield, but Davis ended up starting in most games the rest of the way.

Acquiring former Dodger star Tommy Davis in September was a great deal by the Cubs, but they inexplicably squandered the move by giving him his unconditional release three months later. *National Baseball Hall of Fame Library.*

Acquiring Davis was a great move, but he was another player the Cubs eventually squandered. They inexplicably gave Davis his unconditional release that December. He went to spring training with Oakland in 1971; the A's liked what they saw and signed him, and Davis hit .324 for Oakland that year.

Davis's combined average with Houston, Oakland and the Cubs in 1970 was .284, yet the Cubs released him for reasons known only to management. "Nobody gets released after hitting .284," Davis said.[89] Because the Cubs had released him, Oakland was not bound by the major-league 25 percent limit on salary cuts, and the A's in 1971 paid him less than half of what he had made the previous year, hurting Davis

Cub ace Ferguson Jenkins struggled in the early part of the season but ended up strong and tallied another twenty-win season. *Chicago National League Ball Club Inc. (Chicago Cubs).*

in his wallet both at the time and forever, as the salary reduction affected his pension.[90] Davis's few 1970 weeks with the Cubs, in which he ended up as a starter in most games, therefore negatively impacted the rest of his life.

The Cubs reacquired him for 1972 then traded him to the Baltimore Orioles for Elrod Hendricks (who would hit a whopping .116 for Chicago). From 1973 to 1975, Davis was a full-time player for the Birds, batting .306, .289 and .283—averages that could have helped the Cubs' sub-.500 teams in those years.

Charlie Finley, owner of the A's, got rid of a few of his players that September because Oakland failed to make the playoffs and Finley wanted to dump some salaries. More than Davis, the Cubs needed A's relief pitcher Jim "Mudcat" Grant, 6-2 with twenty-four saves and a 1.82 ERA in Oakland, but they did not go after him. Instead, on September 14, the Pirates got Grant, with the Cubs failing to block the waiver move even though they could have. Grant pitched in eight games for the Pirates down the stretch and won two.

On to Montreal, where the Cubs began a fourteen-game end-of-season road trip. If they were to win the division, they would have to do it away from the Friendly Confines.

They opened the four-game weekend with a Friday, September 18 doubleheader sweep. Jenkins earned his twentieth victory in the opener, 3–2, after attending his fifty-two-year-old mother's funeral.

The nightcap featured some of the oddities seen only in a hot pennant race. Recent acquisition Miller started on the mound for the Cubs, as Durocher announced ahead of time that he planned on employing a spring-training strategy of using several pitchers—Miller, Gura and Colborn—for two innings each. Even more recent acquisition Davis got a pinch-hit that put the Cubs in the lead in the seventh inning, the game went ten innings and Bill Hands relieved in the tenth for the save in his only relief appearance of the year, a 5–4 Cubs victory. The Cubs were now in second place, a game and a half back, as the Pirates beat the Mets to put the New Yorkers two and a half back.

The Cubs won again Saturday, 8–4, but so did the Pirates, who beat the Mets, 2–1, dropping the New Yorkers three and a half back.

On Sunday, the Cubs stumbled, losing to the Expos, 8–4, after having a 4–1 lead in the seventh, with Jenkins making his only relief appearance of the year. The Mets and Pirates split a doubleheader, so now the Cubs were two games back, with the Mets three and a half behind.

Owner Wrigley and vice-president Holland opened the team's wallet again and bought veteran relief pitcher Hoyt Wilhelm from the Atlanta Braves on September 21—months later than they should have, since the Braves never contended in 1970 and would have been amenable to an earlier deal. Wilhelm was well known in Chicago, as he had been the star closer for the White Sox from 1963 to 1968. The Cubs sent Wilhelm right back to the Braves two months later for first baseman Hal Breeden, prompting Major League Baseball's commissioner, Bowie Kuhn, to investigate the deal, as it smacked of one major-league team "borrowing" a player from another.

A Wednesday, September 23 doubleheader at St. Louis severely damaged the Cubs' chances, as their hitting fell asleep and they lost two heartbreakers by the identical scores of 2–1. The opener saw a classic pitching matchup, as Bob Gibson gave up only two hits to beat Ferguson Jenkins. Callison missed the cutoff man on a play in the first game, and Durocher sat him down for the rest of the season in favor of Davis.

In the second game, Williams reached third in the ninth with nobody out as the potential tying run, but the heart of the order—Santo, Hickman and Davis—failed to drive him in. The Cubs dropped another half game behind. They rebounded the next night, 7–1, but remained two and a half back and moved on to Philadelphia for the weekend.

The fifth-place Phillies, as in September 1969, put the nails in the coffin of the Cubs' hopes, beating them 5–3 on Friday; the Cubs fell three and a half back. Durocher decided to bring Hands back on two days' rest on Saturday. The 1940s-style strategy blew up; Hands gave up six runs in only one and two-thirds innings, and the Phillies trounced the Cubs, 7–1, to put them four and a half behind.

Managing to win on Sunday, September 28, 5–3, the Cubs were eliminated anyway as the Pirates beat the Mets, 2–1.

After the game, Durocher showed the strain of the long season. When a reporter asked him when he thought the Cubs lost the pennant, he said: "Opening day. We lost here 2–0." When another reporter asked him who he thought would win the playoffs, Durocher said, "I like the Rams."[91]

The Cubs needed to split the final four games against the Mets in New York to finish second, and they nearly stumbled there, too, losing the first two

Left: Hoyt Wilhelm, star closer for the White Sox from 1963 to 1968, came to the Cubs too late in 1970 to be of much help. *National Baseball Hall of Fame Library*.

Right: The normally genial Ron Santo received death threats on the Cubs' last road trip. The club took the threats so seriously that it sent the third baseman home. *National Baseball Hall of Fame Library*.

games, 6–3 and 3–1, before recovering to take the last two contests of the season, 2–0 and 4–1.

Santo had received some death threats by letter after the 1969 season, but the letters had stopped before spring training in 1970. In September, at the beginning of the final road trip, however, the Wrigley Field switchboard received two death threats against Santo by phone, and the team received one against Santo by letter. Santo bravely played against Montreal, St. Louis and Philadelphia, so long as the Cubs still had a chance. The Office of the Baseball Commissioner and the Cubs even provided security guards for Santo in Philadelphia and New York.

Beckert, Santo's roommate on the road and always a jokester, put a sign above his bed that read, "Beckert sleeps here," and one above Santo's bed, "Santo sleeps here." Beckert told Santo he did not want the would-be assassin to get the wrong guy. He also joked that Popovich should wear Santo's number 10 uniform.

Before the first game against the Mets, Regan went to Santo's room at the hotel to visit, and the security guards pinned the "Vulture" against the wall. At the ballpark, Holland told Santo, "Ron, the security wires at Shea Stadium have been cut."[92]

Since the Cubs had been eliminated by the time the team headed for New York, management just sent him home, and he missed the series. Investigators concluded that the death threats came from someone who had an infatuation with Santo or a person angry at him over 1969, but police never apprehended the perpetrator.

Durocher, ever disdainful of young players, played Popovich at third for all four games of the Met series, despite the Cubs having brought up top third-base prospect Terry Hughes from the minor leagues.

For the second year in a row, the Cubs had sung the "September Song" off-key. Over the final ten games of the season, the Pirates had a win-loss record of 7-3, while the Cubs went only 4-6. In the end, they were 14-14 for the month—not exactly a pennant pace. The Pirates won the division with an 89-73 record, with the Cubs second at 84-78 and the Mets third at 83-79. Had the Cubs matched their 1969 record of 92-70, they would have won the division.

The headline on Jerome Holtzman's end-of-season analysis in the *Sun-Times* read, "Cubs Slow, Cautious, Uninspired."[93]

And on the last day of the month, Ted Abernathy singled home Bobby Floyd in the twelfth inning to give the Kansas City Royals a 14–13 win over the Minnesota Twins. It was pitcher Abernathy's ninth win of the season.

11

OCTOBER

IF ONLY...

In October, rock star Janis Joplin passed away. The comic strip Doonesbury began publishing. Divers found the wreck of the Confederate submarine Hunley in the Atlantic Ocean off South Carolina. The first-ever umpires' strike in Major League Baseball lasted one day. Egyptians elected Anwar Sadat president. And the Cubs finished second in the National League Eastern Division.

s beloved as the 1969 Cubs were, the 1970 Cubs were the better team—and not only because Pappas and Pepitone made the team stronger.

Typically conservative Cub management suddenly became liberal when it came to making moves and spending money. There was no standing pat, as the team would quickly trade for or buy players who management thought the Cubs needed—and just as quickly dump players if they failed to do the job. "Now or never," Cub vice-president John Holland had said, and he lived up to that credo the whole year.

In 1969, Durocher exhausted the regulars by playing them constantly, managing as he did in the 1940s. In 1970, the manager entered the modern era of platooning, and the players were more rested. The platoons consisted of Hickman, James and Pepitone in center field; Callison, Hickman and Williams in right; Williams and Davis in left; Banks, Hickman, Pepitone and Smith at first; Hundley, Martin and Hiatt at catcher; and Popovich spelling Santo, Kessinger and Beckert in the infield. After May, Durocher abandoned the three-man starting rotation. A manager known throughout his career as distrustful of young players, Durocher evolved and, even though he did not particularly want to, in 1970, showed no hesitation putting in youngsters James, Colborn, Decker, Dunegan, Reynolds and Gura for key situations.

Cub pitchers were .500 when it came to shutouts, winning nine and losing nine. But day in and day out, the 1970 starting pitching generally proved no less than superb.

The starting rotation of Jenkins, Holtzman, Hands and Pappas, 1970 edition, can actually be considered the eleventh best in the majors since 1954 using the value over replacement player (VORP) measure. Developed by Baseball Prospectus, an organization devoted to sabermetric analysis, VORP measures a player's value to his team. A pitcher with a VORP of 60, for example, allows 60 fewer runs than a marginal major-league pitcher. In 1970, Jenkins had a VORP of 70.9, Holtzman 60.5, Hands 49.2 and Pappas 28.8, for a total VORP of 494.7, placing that rotation in such illustrious company as the 1993 and 1997–98 Atlanta Braves and the 2011 Philadelphia Phillies.[94]

Jenkins set a Cub pitching strikeout record with 274 and won twenty-one games, and he led the league in complete games. The starting rotation tallied fifty-nine complete games, tops in the league. Hands and Holtzman each won seventeen, and Pappas won ten games in ten weeks. Holtzman struck out 202—the only time in his career he exceeded 200. But the bullpen in late-season games managed to lose fifteen of seventeen games relievers entered with the score tied.[95] The bullpen's ERA was 4.63, good for only tenth in the league, while the starters' ERA was 3.55, a difference of 1.08. No other team in the league came close to this much of a difference.[96]

At the plate, when the Cubs were good, they were great, winning thirty-three of the fifty games that could be considered blowouts for a .660 percentage. But in the one-run games, where teams win or lose championships, they could not do the job, winning only seventeen of thirty-eight for a .447 percentage. Their slugging percentage of .415 was good for second in the league, and their on-base plus slugging (OPS) was .748, good for third in the league. The Cubs' total-base tally of 2,277 was fourth in the league. Batters were both patient and too anxious at the plate, finishing a nice fourth in the National League in walks but an unfortunate third in the league in strikeouts.

Both Billy Williams and Jim Hickman had the best seasons of their careers. Leading the league in games played, runs and hits, with forty-two home runs, a .322 batting average and 129 RBI, Williams finished second

Right: Left-handed starting pitcher Ken Holtzman tallied his career-best season strikeout total with 202 in 1970. *National Baseball Hall of Fame Library*.

Below: Known for his slick fielding, Don Kessinger earned a Gold Glove and led National League shortstops with 501 assists. *National Baseball Hall of Fame Library*.

to Johnny Bench in Most Valuable Player voting and had a better season than Bench. Had the Cubs won their division, Williams likely would have been the MVP. Hickman had thirty-two home runs and a career-best .315 batting average, batted in 115 runs, was tops on the team in on-base percentage with .419 and walks with ninety-three and tallied thirteen game-winning hits. The *Sporting News* named Hickman National League Comeback Player of the Year.

Santo, despite struggling at times at the plate, hit twenty-six home runs and had 114 RBI; Santo, Williams and Hickman gave the Cubs three hitters with more than 100 RBI each for only the second time in the team's history.

Kessinger won the Gold Glove for his superb defense at shortstop. Beckert had made the All-Star team. Pepitone, in only a half season, hit twelve home runs and drove in forty-four.

All-Star Beckert set personal career highs in runs (ninety-nine) and walks (thirty-two), but nonetheless he was dissatisfied with his play that year. "I just don't think I had that good a season," he said. "I wasn't doing the basic things, like getting on base and advancing the runners."[97] The next year, however, he would hit a career-best .342.

Along with winning the Gold Glove, Kessinger led NL shortstops with 501 assists, and he led the team with fourteen triples, most by a Cub since 1944.

Durocher's inability to get along with Callison caused the longtime Philadelphia star to have a mediocre season, hitting .264. Gamble, whom the Cubs dealt to acquire Callison, hit .262 and would have been a big help in the field.

The 1970 Cubs were slow. They seldom tried to steal bases—the Cubs were last in the league with thirty-nine—and when someone other than James or Pepitone played center field, too many balls that should have been outs dropped in for hits. With a total of 137 errors and a .978 fielding percentage, both ranking fourth in the league, the Cubs gave away too many games when they were on defense.

Durocher "provided virtually no inspiration," Jerome Holtzman wrote, adding that Durocher's managerial style was "strictly safety first."[98] Worse, he put too much pressure on the players, according to Langford.[99] If a reliever had a bad outing, as so many of them did that season, Durocher would leave the pitcher languishing in the bullpen for days instead of bringing him right back. When Durocher would finally call on that reliever again, he would be rusty and nervous.

Although he platooned his players more than in the past and had to rely on young pitchers as the bullpen faltered, overall, Durocher still underutilized and stressed the young players. Hughes, who came up from the minors to play for the Cubs in May and September, said: "Leo can really put some pressure on a young kid. He expects you to go out and play without making a mistake. And you are afraid to make a mistake because you will be back in the minors. It's really hard when you have to play that way."[100]

Skidmore went even further. "Leo Durocher was the most intimidating, foul-mouthed, nastiest, arrogant man I have ever met....He didn't like the young players and he let us know it by totally ignoring us."[101]

Had Durocher lost his mental sharpness in 1969 and 1970, as some sportswriters contended? Like any manager, he made some bad moves, but he made some brilliant moves in those seasons as well.

During a game in 1972, with the Cubs having traded Willie Smith after the 1970 season, Durocher yelled to the Cub bench that Smith should get ready to pinch-hit. Hickman rose from the silent bench and told Durocher, "Skip, Willie Smith hasn't been with us for the last two years, but if you want me to, I'll find him and bring him here."[102]

Injuries to Randy Hundley, which put him out of the lineup for seventy-five games, took a serious toll on the Cubs' fortunes. The team was below .500 in games in which Hundley was missing from the lineup. *National Baseball Hall of Fame Library.*

Yet also in 1972, after resigning as Cub manager in midseason and joining the Houston Astros, Durocher managed the Astros to a winning season and then followed up with managing Houston to another winning season in 1973. In fact, Durocher's teams had a losing record in only five of his twenty-five seasons as a manager.

Hundley's injuries, which put him out of the lineup for seventy-five games, took a serious toll on the 1970 Cubs' fortunes. The team was below .500 in games in which Hundley was unavailable. In addition, Durocher relied on Hundley to advise him whether to leave a pitcher in a game or remove him; for almost half the season, that advice was not available.[103]

Durocher said of Hundley: "He meant at least ten games in the standings. No one ran on him when he was catching, and he was a good hitter. They took away more than just a catcher. They took away my general out there."[104] Despite Hundley's limited play, baseball experts rated him the top defensive catcher of 1970—a year in which catcher Johnny Bench of the Cincinnati Reds would win the MVP award.

Baseball writer, historian and statistician Bill James discovered the relationship among runs scored, runs allowed and wins, now known as Pythagorean Win-Loss, since it resembles trigonometry's Pythagorean Theorem.[105] According to Pythagorean Win-Loss, the 1970 Cubs, who scored 806 runs, gave up 679 and finished 84-78, should have finished 94-68, a Pythagorean Win-Loss trigonometry difference of ten games.[106] That should-have-been win-loss record would have had them finish in first place by a comfortable five games over the Pirates. Had the Cubs merely played .500 baseball during their twelve-game June losing streak, eight games of which were decided by three runs or less, they would have finished first at 90-72.

The people certainly supported the club that year, spinning the turnstiles to the tune of 1,642,705 fans in attendance, a number that, at the time, was second only to that of 1969 and higher than the 1970 National League average.

Five future Hall of Famers—Banks, Jenkins, Santo, Wilhelm and Williams—played for the 1970 Cubs, and manager Durocher was a future Hall of Famer as well.

Finishing five games behind the Pirates, the Cubs came closer to first place than they had in any year since they won the National League pennant in 1945, including 1969.

They played 46-34 baseball at home. Unfortunately, they played below .500 on the road (38-44). They also faltered in one-run contests with a record of 17-21, and in extra-inning games, where they were 4-6.

The Cincinnati Reds beat the Pittsburgh Pirates in the National League Championship Series, and the Baltimore Orioles beat the Reds in the World Series.

Would the Cubs have beaten the Cincinnati Reds in the playoffs? Likely, yes, surprisingly. Despite being touted as the Big Red Machine, Cincinnati scored fewer runs than the Cubs (775), allowed more (681) and had a Pythagorean Win-Loss of only 91-71, instead of their actual 102-60 record.[107] The Cubs were one of only two teams in the National League that had a regular-season winning record against the Reds in 1970, with the Cubs taking the season series, 7–5. The Cubs continued playing well against essentially the same Red lineup for several years, finishing at .500

against them in 1971, dominating the pennant-winning 1972 Reds 8–4 and retaining that 8–4 dominance against the Western Division champions in 1973, the last year that the 1970 Cub lineup remained mostly intact. If there was one team the Cubs could consistently beat in those years, it was the Reds.

Would the Cubs have beaten the Baltimore Orioles in the World Series? *Chicago Today*'s Rick Talley certainly thought so, in April predicting the Cubs over the Orioles in seven games.[108] Baltimore scored fewer runs than the Cubs that year, 792 to 806, so the Cub offense could easily match that of the Orioles.

Baltimore had something to prove after losing to the Mets the year before, but so did the Cubs. Pappas also would have had something to prove against the Baltimore team that had let him go five years before. And without some of the horrendous player moves of 1970, fleet-footed, twenty-year-old Gamble would have been available to catch anything hit to the spacious Baltimore outfield and Abernathy and Aguirre would have come out of the bullpen to shut down the Birds' big bats in the late innings.

Whatever the result, a World Series between the Cubs' All-Stars and future Hall of Famers and the Orioles' All-Stars and future Hall of Famers, with two of the greatest managers in history, Durocher and Earl Weaver, in the dugouts, was sure to have been a classic.

But it was not to be.

In the end, the 1970 club never got over 1969. No less of an authority than Ron Santo said, "If we had won in '69, I really do believe we would have won in '70."[109] Ken Holtzman has said the same.[110]

12

1970s AND AFTER

In a season that held such promise, joy and frustration, the 1970 Cubs finished second, five games behind the Pittsburgh Pirates in the National League Eastern Division. They would again finish five games behind, but in fifth place, when the Mets won the division in 1973. The Cubs would not come that close again until they actually won the division in 1984.

But it did not have to be that way.

The 1970 season had a great impact on the team for the rest of the decade, as the Cubs in that year had—and either that year or in subsequent years let go too soon—so many players who would go on to have stellar seasons or great careers for other teams: Abernathy, Colborn, Tommy Davis, Day, Decker, Gura, Gamble, Jestadt, Metzger, Miller and Selma. All Cub management had to do was literally nothing—just keep what they had— and the team would have been a dominant one in the 1970s, instead of a perennial doormat or .500 club.

It also was 1970 that sealed in the psychological expectation in the minds of the players and the fans that somehow, some way, the Cubs were going to collapse. Had they won in 1970, the memory of 1969's collapse would have become a mere footnote in fans' psyches, just as the second-place finishes of the Milwaukee Braves and Chicago White Sox in the 1950s became mental footnotes for their fans once their teams won the pennant. Instead, a Cub collapse became an expectation in 1970, and so it happened again in 1973 and 1977 after the team spent the early parts of those seasons sailing along in first place only to collapse later. And it happened in the 1984 and 2003

National League Championship Series, after the Cubs came within one game of winning the pennant and each time then lost three straight games to let it slip away.

It required a new generation, literally a team full of players not even born in 1970, to finally win it all in 2016.

The team to win it all could have been the 1970 Cubs; a team now forgotten but that might have been one of the best clubs ever seen at Wrigley Field if not for injuries to Hundley, the distraction of Durocher's radio show, the tensions between Durocher and his players, scarred psyches and—most of all—bullpen failures and bad trades.

13
EPILOGUE

Santo and Beckert begged Cub management not to break up the team after 1970, so the Cubs essentially put the same team on the field in 1971, sans Miller, Wilhelm and Tommy Davis—all of whom could have played a beneficial role. After a slow start, the Cubs never contended, finishing in third place, fourteen games behind the Pirates. Pappas led a clubhouse revolt against Durocher, and Santo and the manager nearly came to blows over Durocher's opposition to the Cubs scheduling Ron Santo Day at the request of the Diabetes Association of Chicago. Phil Wrigley took out ads in Chicago's daily newspapers reaffirming his support for Durocher.

After trading Ken Holtzman for Rick Monday and acquiring José Cardenal from Milwaukee for Colborn, and after Banks retired, but with the rest of the team essentially the same as the 1970 squad, the Cubs in 1972 improved to second place with a .548 winning percentage. That was better than the .519 of 1970 and only .001 shy of the Pirates' 1970 division-winning .549 percentage. Durocher stepped down as manager in July.

The 1973 club looked to finally make fans forget the failures of 1969 and 1970, in first place by eight and a half games on June 23, only to finish below .500 in fifth place.

After that epic collapse, management broke up the team, scattering all the stars of 1970 except for Don Kessinger and Billy Williams around both major leagues—and even Kessinger and Williams would be traded within a few years. Beckert, Kessinger, Santo, Hundley and Williams had played together for nine seasons (1965–73); Jenkins had played with them for eight (1966–73);

"I don't think there has ever been a baseball team that has stayed closer together," said Glenn Beckert of the late 1960s–early 1970s Cubs. *National Baseball Hall of Fame Library.*

and Banks had played with them for seven seasons (1965–71). The way free agency and high salaries have restructured baseball, seven players will never spend that much time on the same team again. "I don't think there has ever been a baseball team that has stayed closer together," Beckert said.[111]

"It was a sad end to a glorious run," said Al Kipp, longtime editorial director for DePaul University. "Nevertheless, all of those names remain in my memory."[112]

Gura, Hundley, Holtzman and Jenkins would return to play for the Cubs years later, after their best seasons were behind them.

The Cubs would not contend again until 1977.

Sports journalists and baseball experts talked about several Cubs of the late 1960s and early 1970s becoming major-league managers—Ernie Banks, Randy Hundley and Billy Williams among them—but no team ever came calling for those stars to enter the managerial ranks. Hundley even managed in the Cubs' minor-league system, but when the *Chicago Tribune* and general manager Dallas Green took over the team in the early 1980s, they engaged in another post-1973-like purge, and the Cubs cut Hundley loose. Of the Cubs of that era, Don Kessinger and Phil Regan did end up managing in the majors.

At a team reunion banquet in 1983, Leo Durocher, in front of the whole crowd of former players, had nothing but good things to say about them. And he apologized to Santo, and his family, for the way Durocher had treated the third baseman. "The moving speech by Leo had most of the room in tears," Feldmann wrote.[113]

The Chicago Cubs would finally win a division title in 1984, and the National League pennant and the World Series in 2016—with 1970 long forgotten.

14

WHAT ABOUT THE WEST?

When Major League Baseball first created geographically named divisions before the 1969 season, based on location, the Chicago Cubs and St. Louis Cardinals, who ended up in the National League Eastern Division, should have been in the Western Division with the Houston Astros, Los Angeles Dodgers, San Diego Padres and San Francisco Giants. The Atlanta Braves and Cincinnati Reds, who ended up in the Western Division, should have been in the Eastern Division with the Montreal Expos, New York Mets, Philadelphia Phillies and Pittsburgh Pirates.

Cub and Cardinal management preferred placement in the Eastern Division, however, feeling that they would lose television revenue if too many of their games were played on the West Coast starting at 10:00 p.m. Central Time. They had the clout to make it happen.

This was a mistake. As Major League Baseball commissioner Fay Vincent said in 1992, the Cubs and Cardinals in the Western Division, and the Atlanta Braves and Cincinnati Reds in the East, would have been "in the best interest of baseball."[114]

Arthur Daley wrote in the *New York Times* in the spring of 1969 that the Cubs "could be a winner this season if geographers had placed them in the Western Division. Unfortunately for them, however, they are in the East."[115]

Daley proved right, and not just for 1969.

In 1992, I attempted to project mathematically what all National League teams' records, and the final NL standings, would have been in all the years of divisional play up to that time (1969–91) if the Cubs and Cardinals had been in the Eastern Division and the Braves and Reds in the Western Division.

This was not simply a matter of moving teams' actual records into the other divisions. Since teams at the time played eighteen games against each *intra*-division rival, and twelve games against each *inter*-division rival, I had to mathematically project new records for the four teams against all rivals except the moving teams.

The study starts with a hypothesis: an assumption that the four moving clubs would have achieved similar win-loss percentages against individual clubs over eighteen games as they did over twelve, and over twelve games as they did over eighteen. Based on that, one could project what each team's new record against each individual club might have been, what each season's National League standings might have been, and which teams would have finished with the best records in their divisions.

Such projections showed that in 1969, the New York Mets would have won the Eastern Division with a 100-62 win-loss record, as they had in reality. In the Western Division, however, the Cubs would have finished first with a 96-66 record, rather than their actual 92-70, with a comfortable six-game margin over the second-place Cardinals.[116]

The Mets, therefore, would have played the Cubs in the National League Championship Series, instead of the Atlanta Braves. Who would have won? It is unknown, but at least the Cubs would have won a division and gone to the playoffs and would not have had the monkey of the 1969 collapse on their backs for 1970 and beyond.

According to the mathematical projections, in the Western Division in 1970, Los Angeles would have finished 88-73, and the Cubs one-half game behind at 88-74, necessitating play of a rained-out game between the Dodgers and the Phillies. Had Los Angeles lost this game, the Dodgers and Cubs would have finished tied, and a tiebreaker game would have been required. Even with bad trades and the 1970 Cubs' other problems, they could have gone to the playoffs anyway had they played in the Western Division, facing the Cincinnati Reds, the projected Eastern Division champions, in the National League Championship Series.

The *Delta Epsilon Sigma Journal*'s editors felt this study had merit and ran an article about it in the journal in 1992.

Once again, a bad decision by Cubs' management, putting the team in the Eastern Division, may have cost the team the 1970 National League pennant—and the 1969 pennant as well.

15

WHAT IF?

THE CUBS IN POSTSEASON PLAY

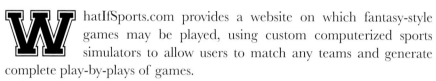 hatIfSports.com provides a website on which fantasy-style games may be played, using custom computerized sports simulators to allow users to match any teams and generate complete play-by-plays of games.

So, what if the Chicago Cubs and Cincinnati Reds had met in the National League Championship Series in 1970? Could the Cubs have made the World Series against the Baltimore Orioles? Running computer simulations on WhatIfSports.com tells us what would have happened.

NLCS GAME ONE

Beautiful Wrigley Field was the site of the opening game of the National League Championship Series on Saturday, October 3, 1970. The weather was partly cloudy and chilly with a high temperature of sixty degrees Fahrenheit for the Cubs' first postseason appearance since 1945.

Both the Cincinnati Reds and the Chicago Cubs started their aces on the mound: Gary Nolan for the Reds and Ferguson Jenkins for the Cubs.

Batting order for the Reds was Pete Rose (RF), Bobby Tolan (CF), Tony Perez (3B), Johnny Bench (C), Lee May (1B), Bernie Carbo (LF), Tommy Helms (2B), Woody Woodward (SS) and Nolan (P).

For the Cubs, it was Don Kessinger (SS), Glenn Beckert (2B), Billy Williams (LF), Ron Santo (3B), Joe Pepitone (CF), Jim Hickman (RF), Ernie Banks (1B), Randy Hundley (C) and Jenkins (P). With John Callison in Durocher's doghouse and fan sentiment calling for Banks to play, it would have been an easy decision for the manager to start Banks at home at first and to put Hickman in right field.

The first inning and a half were uneventful, but in the bottom of the second, Pepitone led off with a solo homer. The Reds got the run right back in the top of the third when Tolan singled, stole second and scored when a Bench drive ricocheted off the glove of Pepitone, who was charged with a two-base error.

The Cubs came charging back in the bottom of the third on a single by Beckert, a two-run homer by Williams, a solo home run by Santo, a double by Pepitone and an RBI single by Hundley. Jenkins's ground-out ended the inning, and the Cubs had a 5–1 lead.

After the Reds scored another run in the top of the fourth to make it 5–2, the Cubs really started flexing their muscle. The bottom of the fourth started off with a Kessinger single. He moved to second on a Beckert sacrifice, and a Williams single drove him in. After a Santo strikeout, Pepitone singled and Hickman hit a three-run homer. Sparky Anderson finally replaced Nolan with Ray Washburn, and the moment Cub fans had been waiting for since 1953 finally happened: Ernie Banks hit a postseason home run. The Cubs' lead was 10–2 after four innings.

They added what looked to be a meaningless run in the bottom of the fifth on hits by Kessinger and Williams for an apparently insurmountable 11–2 lead.

But this was the Big Red Machine, and Cincinnati was not yet done. The Reds added a run in the bottom of the sixth on hits by Woodward, Rose and Tolan to cut the lead to 11–3, and that remained the score through the seventh.

With 313 regular-season innings under Jenkins's belt and an eight-run lead, Durocher decided to give his starter

The computer-generated National League Championship Series predicted that "Mr. Cub" Ernie Banks would have hit a home run in Game One. *National Baseball Hall of Fame Library.*

a rest and brought in rookie Gura, and the manager almost immediately regretted it. The lefthander retired the first batter but then gave up a single. Rose came up and crushed a two-run homer to left-center field, cutting the lead to 11–5. That was enough for Durocher, who did not like rookies anyway, and the manager replaced Gura with veteran Phil Regan, who retired Tolan and Perez to end the inning.

With a six-run lead in the top of the ninth inning, Cubs fans' worst fears about their shaky bullpen came to fruition. Regan came out again to pitch and promptly gave up a solo homer to Bench. 11–6. The Vulture struck out May but got the hook after Carbo hit a double. Juan Pizarro came in and gave up a single to Helms and an RBI single to Woodward, Carbo scoring. 11–7.

No doubt wishing Hoyt Wilhelm had been acquired early enough to be on the postseason roster, manager Durocher quickly removed Pizarro and brought in Roberto Rodriguez to pitch. Cub fans breathed a little easier when Rodriguez struck out pinch-hitter Hal McRae. Rose then hit a fly ball to Pepitone in center that should have been the game-ender, but shades of Matty Alou, Pepitone botched it, putting Rose on base with an error and Helms scoring. 11–8. The rattled Rodriguez threw a wild pitch with Tolan at bat, allowing Woodward to score before Tolan hit an RBI single to drive in Rose and make the score 11–10.

Durocher's hunch manager persona came out as he continued to stick with Rodriguez. His faith was rewarded as Rodriguez noticed Tolan taking too big a lead off first. The pitcher threw a pickoff toss to Banks, Tolan took off for second and Mr. Cub's throw to Kessinger easily put Tolan out, ending the game. Cubs 11, Reds 10.

How realistic is the WhatIfSports.com Game 1 scenario? Very. The Cubs were second in the league in scoring with 806 runs, and the Reds were third with 775, so an 11–10 game is not surprising. Neither is the Cubs' shaky Abernathy-less bullpen blowing an 11–2 lead. And neither is Billy Williams being the player of the game by driving in four runs.

NLCS Game Two

The temperaments of Red manager Sparky Anderson and volatile Cub manager Leo Durocher could not have been more different. Whereas in 1969 Don Young's game-losing miscues against the Mets aroused Durocher's anger enough to sit Young down the next game, Anderson showed his confidence in Tolan by starting the outfielder again in Game 2 despite his game-losing base-running blunder.

Sunday, October 4, was slightly warmer at sixty-six degrees, with the sun again coming in and out from behind the clouds all day long in Chicago.

Anderson slightly altered the Reds' lineup, starting Hal McRae in left field, batting sixth and replacing Carbo. The manager tabbed Jim Merritt as the starting pitcher. Durocher kept the same lineup as the day before, with Ken Holtzman getting the start.

The Cubs once again looked good at the plate, scoring three runs in the first on singles by Williams, Santo, Pepitone, Hickman and Banks. The score remained 3–0 until the top of the third, when Rose, Tolan and Perez singled, Bench walked and May and McRae singled to give Cincinnati a 4–3 lead.

The Reds increased their lead in the fourth when Rose singled and then was doubled in by Tolan, who moved to third on a groundout by Perez. Bench hit a sacrifice fly to drive in Tolan, and May hit a solo homer to stretch the lead to 7–3. Although Durocher had hoped to avoid going to the bullpen, particularly after his relievers had poured gasoline on the fire the day before, he removed Holtzman and again brought in Gura, who retired McRae on a groundout. The Cubs got one back in the bottom of the frame on a Hundley single and Beckert double to cut the lead to 7–4.

Gura started the top of the fifth strong by retiring Helms on a groundout. After Woodward singled, Merritt popped out to Hundley. But then Rose and Tolan both singled, bringing Perez up—who promptly hit a grand slam to make the score 11–4. That was all for Gura, whom Durocher replaced with Jim Colborn, who ended the inning by striking out Bench. The Cubs tallied one more in the home half on singles by Pepitone, Hickman and Hundley to make the score 11–5.

The Cubs continued to fight back in the bottom of the sixth, with Kessinger and Beckert singling and Santo driving in Kessinger on a force out. With Merritt tiring, Anderson replaced him with Ray Washburn, who gave up a single to Pepitone and an RBI single to Hickman before retiring Banks on a fly out to cut the Reds' lead to 11–7.

In the home half of the seventh, John Callison pinch-hit for Colborn and started a rally with a single. Washburn hit Kessinger with a pitch, Williams walked, and Santo singled to drive in Callison. Anderson went to his bullpen again, bringing in Don Gullett, who promptly uncorked a wild pitch, scoring Kessinger. Gullett got Pepitone to ground out, and the score was a tight 11–9.

Regan took the mound for the Cubs in the eighth in an uneventful inning for both teams. After two outs for the Reds in the top of the ninth, Rose reached on a Beckert error, Tolan singled and the unstoppable Perez hit another home run, this time driving in three runs for a 14–9 Red lead, which turned out to be the final score. The NLCS was tied at a game apiece, making it the first LCS ever to be assured of going more than three games.

Although the Reds and the Cubs pounded out eighteen hits apiece, the difference was that only one Cub hit, a double by Beckert, was for extra bases. Perez, with two home runs and eight RBI, was easily the player of the game.

Once again, WhatIfSports.com could be considered accurate, with both the Reds and Cubs able to score big and the Cub bullpen ineffective.

NLCS GAME THREE

On to Cincinnati for Game Three on Monday, October 5, on a seventy-eight-degree sunny day. For the Reds, Carbo was back in left field, McRae was back on the bench and veteran Tony Cloninger was on the mound. For the Cubs, with Banks hitting only .200 and having only limited range on artificial turf, and Callison coming through with a pinch-hit the day before, Durocher slightly altered his lineup with Callison in right field batting seventh and Hickman moving to first base. Bill Hands was the starting pitcher.

The Cubs took command in the top of the first, with Pepitone singling in Kessinger, who had walked, for the visitors' first run, and Hickman hitting a three-run homer for a 4–0 lead that the Cubs would never relinquish. In the fourth inning, a Hickman single drove in Beckert for Gentleman Jim's fourth RBI of the day and player-of-the-game honors. Hands, who had been considered the Cubs' stopper in both 1969 and 1970, shut down the Reds and won the game, 9–2, with bullpen help from Gura and Colborn.

NLCS GAME FOUR

With a two-games-to-one lead in the best-of-five NLCS, the Cubs were hoping to wrap up the pennant in Riverfront Stadium in Game Four. With Milt Pappas on the mound, who had pitched a superb 1–0 shutout against the Big Red Machine on July 23, and who had a grudge to settle with a team for which he had not enjoyed playing, Cub fans were confident. Jim McGlothlin took the mound for the Reds.

The Cubs started out strong in the top of the first again with a solo home run by Billy Williams. That was the last run the Cubs would score all day, however, as McGlothlin threw eight strong innings in which the Cubs got only three more hits. Gullett, who had not given up a run in the entire LCS, shut the door on the Cubs in the ninth. The Reds tied the game in the bottom of the first on a Rose single and a Tolan double and took the lead for good in the third on a two-out, three-run double by Lee May, the player of the game. Pappas gave up four runs on the day and Regan one more as the Cubs lost, 5–1.

The 1970 National League pennant would therefore be determined by the results of Game Five.

NLCS GAME FIVE

Would the final game of the NLCS in Cincinnati be a slugfest or a pitchers' duel? Both teams had their aces, Jenkins and Nolan, back on the mound, but both teams had been hot at the plate throughout the series.

As in every other 1970 NLCS game, the Cubs scored first. Kessinger walked and advanced to second on a Beckert sacrifice. After a Williams fly out, Santo singled in the first run.

The score remained 1–0 until the top of the third, when the Cubs took command. After the Cubs had already scored two, Santo, batting only .200 in the series as the day began, jacked a two-run homer to give the Cubs a 5–0 lead. In the top of the fourth, Jenkins, one of the best hitting pitchers in the league, stroked a double down the left-field line but did not score.

A Tolan home run in the bottom of the fourth cut the lead to 5–1, but then the Cubs blew the game open in the top of the sixth, scoring five runs, including another Santo two-run homer to make it 10–1 Cubs.

Santo was player of the game, but he shared the spotlight with Callison. Hitting only .143 as the day began, Callison doubled in Hickman for another run, and in the ninth, Callison hit a two-run homer to put the Cubs up, 13–1.

So it came down to the bottom of the ninth, with Jenkins, who had pitched a league-leading twenty-four complete games in 1970, still on the mound for the Cubs. He quickly retired Perez on a groundout to Kessinger, but the Big Red Machine was not done yet.

Bench hit a hot one to Beckert, who fumbled the ball for an error. May singled to center, and Carbo lined a single to left center, with Bench scoring. After a Helms fly out, Woodward reached base when Jenkins hit him with an inside fastball.

With the bases loaded, Manager Sparky Anderson sent up pitch-hitter Ty Cline. Durocher had nobody up in the Cub bullpen. It was up to Jenkins.

Cline hit a ground ball to Santo, who threw to Hickman at first to retire the last Red batter. Unexpectedly, the Big Red Machine had lost in a blowout, 13–2, and the Chicago Cubs were 1970 National League champions!

The Cubs did it with starting pitchers Jenkins (2-0, 2.81 ERA) and Hands (1.0, 1.29 ERA) and their hitting. Kessinger hit .318; Beckert, an incredible .526; Williams, .391 with two homers; Santo, .300 with three dingers; Pepitone, .363 with one home run; Hickman, .400 with two homers; and Callison, .273 with one four-bagger. Hundley had an off series at the plate with .211, and Banks hit only .167 but with one home run. Gura and Regan were generally ineffective out of the pen, but Colborn and Rodriguez gave up no earned runs, and Rodriguez earned a save.

The Cubs' flight to Chicago was met by hundreds of fans when it landed, and the team looked forward to opening the 1970 World Series at Beautiful Wrigley Field.

WORLD SERIES GAME ONE

The temperature was only in the high fifties, but the weather was clear on Saturday, October 10 in Chicago's Wrigley Field for the opening game of the 1970 World Series featuring the Baltimore Orioles and Chicago Cubs. Jim Palmer, at 20-10 with a 2.71 ERA during the regular season, took the mound for Baltimore. With Ferguson Jenkins having pitched the last game of the NLCS, Ken Holtzman, who had been shelled in Game Two of the playoffs, was the starting pitcher for the Cubs.

Manager Earl Weaver's batting order for the Orioles was Don Buford (LF), Paul Blair (CF), Boog Powell (1B), Frank Robinson (RF), Brooks Robinson (3B), Elrod Hendricks (C), Dave Johnson (2B), Mark Belanger (SS) and Palmer (P).

For the Cubs, it was Don Kessinger (SS), Glenn Beckert (2B), Billy Williams (LF), Ron Santo (3B), Joe Pepitone (CF), Jim Hickman (RF), Ernie Banks (1B), Randy Hundley (C) and Holtzman (P). Although Callison had had a better NLSC than Banks, manager Durocher knew he would be run out of town if he failed to start Banks in the Cubs' first World Series game at Wrigley Field since 1945.

The Orioles had been the highest-scoring team in the American League in 1970 with 792 runs during the regular season. The Cubs had actually outscored them with 806, but both teams' bats were as cold as the weather in the series opener as Palmer and Holtzman engaged in a classic pitchers' duel.

Baltimore threatened in the top of the second when Hendricks blooped a double to right field with two outs and Holtzman walked Johnson. Belanger then hit a shallow fly out to right, however, and the Orioles failed to score.

After that, both pitchers settled down and dominated their opponents. After the seventh-inning stretch, Santo led off, Palmer made his first mistake of the day and Santo crushed a solo homer to left field for a 1–0 Cub lead.

In the top of the eighth, Belanger lined one off Kessinger's glove for an infield single. Merv Rettenmund pinch-hit for Palmer and struck out, but then Buford doubled to right for runners on second and third. Durocher had no intention of going to his shaky bullpen, and Holtzman got Blair to ground out to Santo with the runners holding. Holtzman then struck out Powell to end the threat.

The Cub lefty retired the two Robinsons and Hendricks one-two-three in the ninth inning for a 1–0 shutout—the first in the World Series since Oriole pitchers tallied two in the 1966 Fall Classic. Holtzman gave up only five hits and was player of the game.

WORLD SERIES GAME TWO

The players woke up to temperatures in the thirties on the morning of Sunday, October 11, but by game time in the afternoon, the thermometer rose to the mid-fifties. Both starting lineups other than pitchers were the same as in Game One, with Mike Cuellar (24-8 with a 3.48 ERA in the regular season) taking the mound for the Orioles and Bill Hands, who had won Game Three of the NLCS, pitching for the Cubs.

For the sixth straight postseason game, the Cubs took the early lead. In the bottom of the first, a Beckert single and a home run by Santo brought in two runs for a 2–0 lead. Cub fans were thrilled in the fourth when, after a Hickman double, Banks had the moment they had been waiting for, hitting a two-run homer to make the score 4–0. Pepitone's solo homer in the fifth made it 5–0. Hands sailed along as he had done in Game Three of the NLCS, shutting out the Orioles for seven innings. But after he gave up a run with two outs in the top of the eighth, Durocher brought in Regan, who retired Frank Robinson to end the inning.

The Cubs looked to have the game wrapped up in the top of the ninth, but shades of the ninth inning of Game One of the NLCS, the bullpen once again proved to be an arson squad. The Oriole rally started with a Brooks Robinson double and a Hendricks walk, so Durocher yanked Regan in favor of Pizarro. Johnson promptly doubled, scoring Robinson. 5–2. Pizarro retired Belanger on a fly out, but then pinch-hitter Terry Crowley singled, scoring Hendricks. With the score 5–3, Durocher brought in Rodriguez to face Buford, who singled to drive in Johnson, trimming the lead to 5–4.

That brought up Paul Blair, who jacked a line-drive, three-run homer to center field, putting the jubilant Orioles ahead, 7–5, in front of more than thirty-seven thousand dejected, deflated, disbelieving Cub fans.

With little left to lose, Durocher brought in Gura, whose ERA in the NLCS had been a staggering 47.38. The rookie lefthander proved he could meet the challenge, however, immediately getting Powell to ground out. After walking Frank Robinson, Gura retired Brooks Robinson on a fly out to Hickman.

Eddie Watt entered the game to pitch for the Orioles in the Cub ninth. Beckert, coming off a hot NLCS, singled to center. Williams, also a 1970

Computer-generated World Series Game Two resulted in Ron Santo hitting two home runs for the Cubs. *Chicago History Museum, ICHi-065786.*

postseason star, singled to right. Managers of that era such as Baltimore's Earl Weaver often trusted their pitchers to work out of a jam, so Watt remained in the game as Ron Santo strode to the plate.

To the Orioles' shock, Santo, already with a first-inning four-bagger to his credit, crushed a three-run, walk-off homer down the left-field line to turn what looked to be a depressing Cub loss into an 8–7 victory, capping one of the wildest ninth innings in Fall Classic history.

The Cubs then headed to Baltimore with a two-game World Series margin.

World Series Game Three

Southpaw Dave McNally, who had tied for the major-league lead with twenty-four victories, took to the mound in perfect weather in front of a Memorial Stadium crowd of 51,773 to try to pitch the Orioles back into the series. Milt Pappas was thrilled to take the hill for the Cubs, looking to beat the team that had given up on him when Oriole management traded him to Cincinnati in 1966.

Weaver made a few changes to his O's lineup, moving Belanger up to bat second instead of eighth, dropping Blair from the second spot to the fifth spot to get his power into the middle of the order and moving Brooks Robinson from fifth to sixth. Andy Etchebarren started at catcher instead of Hendricks and batted eighth.

Durocher played his "road" lineup, sitting Banks and replacing him in the lineup with right-fielder Callison, with Hickman starting at first base.

Baltimore's new lineup paid immediate dividends. For the first time in the 1970 postseason, the Cubs' opponents scored first, as Don Buford and Frank Robinson crossed the plate on a double by Blair for a 2–0 Oriole lead after an inning.

The Cubs got one back in the top of the second, but the Orioles scored once in the third and then tallied three more in the fourth when Powell broke out of his series slump with a two-run homer. Frank Robinson followed with another four-bagger for a 6–1 Baltimore lead. A Blair home run in the seventh made the score 7–1 Orioles.

The Cub eighth started off uneventfully with two quick outs, but then the inning became a repeat of Game Two's Oriole ninth. Beckert singled and Williams tripled. 7–2. Santo singled, driving in Williams. 7–3. That was all for McNally, and Pete Richert entered the game. Pepitone doubled, Hickman walked and Callison singled, driving in two runs. 7–5. The rattled Richert uncorked a wild pitch to score Hickman before settling down and getting Hundley to ground out. Orioles 7, Cubs 6.

Rettenmund pinch-hit for Richert in the bottom of the eighth, requiring Weaver to change pitchers for the top of the ninth. Trusting in Watt despite the Game Two debacle, Weaver was rewarded when pinch-hitter Banks, hitting for pitcher Gura, and Kessinger both grounded out. Everyone in Memorial Stadium was shocked, however, when Beckert, with only three home runs during the regular season, hit a solo home run to tie the game at seven, bringing the Orioles up in an unexpected bottom of the ninth inning.

Regan entered the game to pitch for the Cubs in the Oriole ninth and immediately encountered trouble. Frank Robinson led off with a single. Regan retired the dangerous Blair on a pop-up to Kessinger, but then Brooks Robinson singled. That was all Durocher could stand, and he replaced Regan with Rodriguez, who promptly struck out Johnson. Etchebarren, the Orioles' backup catcher, became a World Series surprise hero by singling in Frank Robinson for a wild 8–7 Oriole win.

As it had so often during 1970, in the WhatIfSports.com scenario, the Cub bullpen failed once again. But the Cubs still held a 2-1 World Series lead.

World Series Game Four

Despite Etchebarren's heroics, Weaver returned to his regular lineup on October 14 for Game Four, putting Hendricks back behind the plate and bringing back Palmer to be the moundsman as in the opener. Jenkins took the hill for the Cubs for his first-ever World Series appearance in front of 53,007 in Memorial Stadium on a crystal-clear, eighty-two-degree day. Callison once again started in right field for the Cubs.

It was the Cubs' day, particularly Callison's. The right-fielder started off the scoring with a solo home run in the third, then doubled in Hickman in the fifth and scored on a surprise two-run Jenkins homer for a 4–0 Cub lead. Callison got another RBI in the sixth to make the score 5–0 Cubs.

After the Orioles scratched for a run in the seventh, the Cubs turned the game into a blowout by scoring four in the eighth, three of them on a Callison homer. Jenkins went all the way for a 9–2 complete-game victory to put the Cubs one game away from being world's champions.

WORLD SERIES GAME FIVE

Weaver hoped that the Orioles would heat up as the temperature cooled to sixty-nine degrees on a day in which rain threatened, and he shook up his lineup for Game Five in front of 45,341 fans at Memorial Stadium. Belanger (SS) led off, followed by Blair (CF), Frank Robinson (RF) moving up to third in the order, Powell (1B) batting cleanup, Rettenmund getting a start in left field batting fifth, Brooks Robinson (3B) batting sixth, Johnson (2B) in his usual number-seven spot, Etchebarren (the hero of the O's only World Series victory so far) back in the lineup at catcher batting eighth and Cuellar back on the mound.

Durocher stayed with the same hot Cub lineup and brought back Holtzman, the hero of Game One, as the starting pitcher.

The teams traded runs in the second inning as Hickman scored when Hundley grounded into a double play, and Powell immediately tied the game with a solo homer. Pepitone homered in the fourth to give the Cubs a lead of 3–1, which remained the score as Holtzman for the Cubs and first Cuellar and then Richert for the Orioles pitched scoreless ball through the eighth.

In the top of the ninth, Watt relieved Richert and gave up a walk to Hickman. Callison then hit his second home run in as many days, and the Cubs' nervous 3–1 lead suddenly became a comfortable 5–1.

In the bottom of the ninth, Holtzman easily retired pinch-hitter Terry Crowley on a lineout to Hickman and struck out Belanger. But then the unstoppable Blair doubled into center field, and a rattled Holtzman walked Frank Robinson.

With the Cubs' starting pitching much more reliable than their bullpen, Durocher left Holtzman in for a classic confrontation with Powell, who had already homered in the second inning. But this time, Holtzman got the better of the slugger as Powell grounded to Kessinger, who threw to Hickman at first for the final out.

The Chicago Cubs were the World Series Champions of 1970!

In the World Series, at the plate, Kessinger (.174), Beckert (.208) and Hundley (.105) were cold. But the heart of the order made up for them: Williams (.381), Santo (.441, with eight RBIs and three home runs), Pepitone (.353 with two home runs), Hickman (.333) and Callison (an incredible .545 with two home runs in only three games). Banks hit only .125 but also slammed the World Series homer of Cub fans' dreams.

Among moundsmen, Holtzman, by winning two complete games with an 0.50 ERA, was World Series MVP. Jenkins was strong in his one start, winning a complete game and giving up only two runs. Gura was the star out of the bullpen with a victory in relief and an ERA of 0.00.

What if that had actually happened? The Cubs never would have gained the "lovable losers" image—they would have been world champions and maybe would even have won another pennant or two. There never would have been any breakup of the team after the 1973 season—Cub favorites such as Williams, Santo and Jenkins probably would have finished their careers with the team.

And Cub fans would have remembered the 1970 team forever. They would not be the Forgotten Chicago Cubs of 1970.

EDITOR'S NOTE: The Cincinnati Reds' starting lineups for the first three playoff games, and the Baltimore Orioles' starting lineups for the five World Series games, were the actual lineups from the real-life 1970 NLCS and World Series. Results for batters and games courtesy WhatIfSports.com.

16

THE 1970 CHICAGO CUBS

PITCHERS

37 Ted Abernathy, 0-0, 2.00 ERA, 1 save

Ted Abernathy's last year in the majors was with the Kansas City Royals in 1972. In retirement, he worked at Summey Building Systems, a module home company, and in landscaping in Dallas, North Carolina. Abernathy also enjoyed working on cars. He died on December 16, 2004, at age seventy-one.

34 Hank Aguirre, 3-0, 4.50 ERA, 1 save

Hank Aguirre's 1970 season with the Cubs was his last as a pitcher. He coached for the Cubs from 1972 to 1974 and managed in the Oakland Athletics' system in 1975 and 1976. After baseball, Aguirre began a Detroit auto parts manufacturing and supply company, Mexican Industries. The U.S. Hispanic Chamber of Commerce named him Businessman of the Year in 1987. He also became a community activist and attempted to buy the Detroit Tigers in 1990. He died on September 5, 1994, at age sixty-three.

46 Steve Barber, 0-1, 9.53 ERA

Steve Barber's last year as a pitcher was 1974 with the San Francisco Giants. After retiring from baseball, he owned a car-stereo business and an auto-care shop, managed an auto dealership and drove a school bus. He died on February 4, 2007, at age sixty-eight.

48 Jim Colborn, 3-1, 3.59 ERA, 4 saves

Jim Colborn won twenty games and made the All-Star team in 1973 for the Milwaukee Brewers, and he won eighteen for the Kansas City Royals in 1977. One of his fellow pitchers for the Royals in 1977 and 1978 was 1970 Cub teammate Larry Gura. Colborn's last year was 1978, when he pitched for Kansas City and Seattle. After retiring as a player, he coached for the Los Angeles Dodgers, Pittsburgh Pirates and Texas Rangers and served as minor-league coordinator of instruction for the Cubs. He also owned the Ventura County Gulls in the California League.

32 Jim Cosman, 0-0, 27.00 ERA

Jim Cosman's last year as a pitcher was with the Cubs in 1970. Starting as a truck driver for Browning Ferris Waste Industries after his baseball career ended, he became regional vice-president and later served as president and chief operating officer for Republic Services. He died on January 7, 2013, at age sixty-nine.

36 Joe Decker, 2-7, 4.64 ERA

Joe Decker's last year as a major-league pitcher was with the Seattle Mariners in 1979. He had won sixteen games as a starter for the Minnesota Twins in 1974. He also worked as a pitching coach in the Mariner and Tigers systems. Outside of professional baseball, Decker worked in sales, health and nutrition distribution, environmental screening and student counseling. He also coached baseball, softball and flag football. He died on March 2, 2003, at age fifty-five.

32, 34 Jim Dunegan, 0-2, 4.73 ERA

Jim Dunegan began in the minor leagues as an outfielder/first baseman and was a top prospect as a hitter, leading the Cubs' minor-league affiliate, Tacoma, in triples in 1969. His penchant for striking out, however, caused him to think about switching to pitcher, and he made the Cubs' roster in 1970 as a moundsman. That was his last year in the major leagues. He died on October 20, 2014, at age sixty-seven.

40 Larry Gura, 1-3, 3.79 ERA, 1 save

Larry Gura had a long career with the Kansas City Royals, including an 18-10 season with the pennant-winning Kansas City Royals in 1980, a year in which he also was named to the American League All-Star team. He also won eighteen in 1982 and was the Royals' Pitcher of the Year twice. For a while, he and fellow 1970 Cub teammate Jim Colborn served on the Royals' pitching staff together. Gura's last year as a pitcher was 1985, back with the Cubs.

49 Bill Hands, 18-15, 3.70 ERA, 1 save

The Cubs traded Bill Hands, whom the Chicago baseball writers had named Chicago Player of the Year in 1969, to the Minnesota Twins in 1972. His last year in the majors was with the Texas Rangers in 1975. In retirement, he operated a fuel-oil company and ran a gas station in Orient, New York. He died in 2017 at age seventy-six.

30 Ken Holtzman, 17-11, 3.38 ERA

Ken Holtzman was one of the top pitchers in the American League from 1972 to 1975, winning eighteen games or more each year, including twenty-one in 1973, and pitching the Oakland Athletics to three world championships. His last major-league season was back with the Cubs in 1979. In retirement, he worked as a stockbroker and an insurance agent.

31 Ferguson Jenkins, 22-16, 3.39 ERA

The Cubs traded Ferguson Jenkins after the 1973 season, though he returned to pitch for the team in 1982 and 1983. He is the only pitcher in history to notch three thousand strikeouts with fewer than one thousand walks. Jenkins earned the Cy Young Award in 1971. He won twenty games in seven different seasons. The National Baseball Hall of Fame inducted him in 1991. Jenkins devotes his life to charitable work, particularly through the Fergie Jenkins Foundation, and he has written several books.

45 Bob Miller, 0-0, 5.00 ERA, 2 saves

An original 1962 New York Met, Bob Miller finished his career in 1974 back with New York. In 1971, pitching briefly for the Cubs and mostly for the San Diego Padres and Pittsburgh Pirates, Miller won eight games and saved ten with a 1.64 ERA. As the manager of the double-A Amarillo Gold Sox in 1976, he led the team to the league championship. Miller also later served as the pitching coach for the Toronto Blue Jays and the San Francisco Giants and as a scout for the Giants. He died on August 6, 1993, from an auto accident at age fifty-four.

32 Milt Pappas, 10-8, 2.68 ERA

Milt Pappas's last major-league season was with the Cubs in 1973. On the final day of that season, in what was supposed to be a doubleheader, Pappas was scheduled to pitch in the second game and seek his 100th National League victory (to go along with his 110 in the American), but umpires canceled the game. In retirement, he worked as a sports reporter for WLS-TV in Chicago, coached baseball at North Central College in Naperville, Illinois, and was employed in sales. He died on April 19, 2016, at age seventy-six.

46 Juan Pizarro, 0-0, 4.60 ERA, 1 save

Juan Pizarro finished his major-league career with the Pittsburgh Pirates in 1974. He later served as a coach with the Santurce Cangregeros in Puerto Rico and the Rockford Cubs of the Midwest League, and he worked for Santurce Parque Central. He died on February 18, 2021, at age eighty-four.

27 Phil Regan, 5-9, 4.76 ERA, 12 saves

Phil Regan's last year in the majors was with the Chicago White Sox in 1972. He was the last of the 1970 Cubs to wear a major-league uniform, as the New York Mets' pitching coach in 2019 at the age of eighty-two. He has coached at Grand Valley State University in Michigan, with the Seattle Mariners and Cleveland Indians and in 1995 managed the Baltimore Orioles.

39 Archie Reynolds, 0-2, 6.60 ERA

Archie Reynolds led the Texas League in victories in 1968 and spent a good part of 1970 with the Cubs. They traded him to the California Angels in 1970, and he ended his major-league career with the Milwaukee Brewers in 1972. He pitched in the minor leagues in 1973 and 1974. He later worked in Saudi Arabia, testing oil and gas wells for Otis Engineering, and he operated a nightclub in Louisiana.

43 Roberto Rodriguez, 3-2, 5.82 ERA, 2 saves

Roberto Rodriguez finished his major-league career with the Cubs in 1970. He played in the minor leagues through 1974 and in the Venezuelan League through 1979. He also served as a pitching coach and baseball instructor in Venezuela and is in the Venezuelan Baseball Hall of Fame. He died on September 23, 2012, at age seventy-one.

39 Hoyt Wilhelm. 0-1, 9.82 ERA, 0 saves

One of the top relief pitchers of all time, Hoyt Wilhelm pitched his last games in the majors for the Los Angeles Dodgers in 1972 at age forty-nine. He later coached and managed in the minor leagues. In 1985, he became the first relief pitcher inducted into the National Baseball Hall of Fame. Wilhelm had always been considered an older major leaguer; at his passing, it was discovered that his birthday was actually a year before that which had always been reported. He died on August 23, 2002, at age eighty.

Catchers

21 Jack Hiatt, .242, 2 HR, 22 RBI

Jack Hiatt in 1969 had tied Ernie Banks's NL record of seven RBIs in one game. He ended his major-league career with the California Angels in 1972. After retiring, he managed in the minor leagues for the Cubs, Angels, Houston Astros and San Francisco Giants. Hiatt also served as the Giants' director of player development for sixteen years.

9 Randy Hundley, .244, 7 HR, 36 RBI

After stints in Minnesota and San Diego, Gold Glove catcher Randy Hundley returned to the Cubs for his last two seasons in the majors, 1976 and 1977. He eventually required an artificial hip and managed Cub minor-league teams in the late 1970s and early 1980s. Hundley invented and continues to run a major-league fantasy camp for fans, a concept since copied by several other major-league teams.

12 J.C. Martin, .156, 1 HR, 4 RBI

J.C. Martin stayed with the Cubs as a player through the 1972 season. He served as the Cubs' bullpen coach in 1974 and then broadcast Chicago White Sox games on WSNS-TV in 1975.

8, 15 Ken Rudolph, .100, 0 HR, 2 RBI

Ken Rudolph's last season was 1977 with the Baltimore Orioles. He has worked as the head varsity baseball coach at Arcadia High School in Phoenix, Arizona, and as an operations manager for United Parcel Service.

INFIELDERS

14 Ernie Banks, .252, 12 HR, 44 RBI

"Mr. Cub" Ernie Banks's last year as a player was with the Cubs in 1971. He served as a coach and goodwill ambassador for the Cubs for two decades and joined the Cubs' board of directors. He had been a fourteen-time All-Star and won the Most Valuable Player award twice. The National Baseball Hall of Fame inducted him in 1977. Banks also worked in sports marketing, trucking, banking and auto sales. Major League Baseball named Banks, Honus Wagner and Cal Ripken Jr. as the shortstops on its All-Century Team in 1999. Banks earned the Presidential Medal of Freedom in 2013. He died on January 23, 2015, at age eighty-three.

18 Glenn Beckert, .288, 3 HR, 36 RBI

Glenn Beckert was a four-time All-Star, shipped by the Cubs to San Diego for Jerry Morales in the Cubs' post-1973 player purge. The Padres gave Beckert his unconditional release after he hurt his arm; Major League Baseball rules prevent releasing an injured player, so an arbitrator awarded him $35,000 in back pay. That, however, killed Beckert's arrangement with Ray Kroc, owner of the Padres and McDonald's, for Beckert to get a McDonald's franchise. He later became a grain trader at the Chicago Board of Trade. He died on April 12, 2020, at age seventy-nine.

19 Phil Gagliano, .150, 0 HR, 5 RBI

Phil Gagliano's last season was 1974 with the Cincinnati Reds. After retirement, he worked as a salesman for Paramount Liquors and hardware manufacturer Durbin Durco Inc. as operations manager. He died on December 20, 2016, at age seventy-four.

23 Adrian Garrett, .000, 0 HR, 0 RBI

Adrian Garrett's last year in the majors as a player was 1976 with the California Angels. He then became a star with the Hiroshima Carp in

Japan, hitting 102 home runs in three seasons. With Garrett, the Carp won the Japan Series in 1979. Playing in the Venezuela Winter League, Garrett set a record by hitting safely in twenty-eight consecutive games. He has served several American teams' organizations as a coach and minor-league manager, most recently the Cincinnati Reds.

17 Terry Hughes, .333, 0 HR, 0 RBI

The Cubs' number-one selection in the 1967 draft, Terry Hughes finished his major-league career with the Boston Red Sox in 1974. In retirement, he worked as a physical education teacher and baseball coach in Spartanburg, South Carolina.

11 Don Kessinger, .266, 1 HR, 39 RBI

Don Kessinger spent his last year in the major leagues in 1979 as player-manager of the Chicago White Sox. He later served as head baseball coach and assistant to the athletic director at the University of Mississippi and serves as president of Kessinger Real Estate in Oxford, Mississippi. Recipient of many postcareer awards, including induction in the Arkansas and Mississippi Sports Halls of Fame, he is most proud of the Danny Thompson Memorial Award, given to a player who most exemplifies the Christian spirit in Major League Baseball.

16 Roger Metzger, .000, 0 HR, 0 RBI

Roger Metzger was the Houston Astros' starting shortstop from 1972 to 1976, leading the National League in triples in 1971 and 1973. A 1979 table-saw accident cost him the tips of four fingers on his right hand, and he finished his major-league career with the San Francisco Giants in 1980. He also has coached for the Giants.

22 Paul Popovich, .253, 4 HR, 20 RBI

Paul Popovich, nicknamed "The Iceman" by his teammates because of his coolness under pressure, batted .600 in the 1974 National League

Championship Series with the Pittsburgh Pirates, to whom the Cubs traded him in the post-1973 player purge. His last year was with the Pirates in 1975. Popovich later served as a minor-league coach for the Los Angeles Dodgers.

10 Ron Santo, .267, 26 HR, 114 RBI

Ron Santo was traded to the crosstown White Sox in the Cubs' post-1973 player purge. He played for the Sox in 1974 and decided to retire. He took a job as vice-president of sales at Torco Oil and eventually became a hugely popular Cub radio broadcaster, spending twenty years in the booth. Santo was the last unreconstructed Chicago Cub, disdaining the 1969 Mets for the rest of his life and refusing to play in an old-timers' game against them. He died at age seventy on December 2, 2010, and was posthumously elected to the National Baseball Hall of Fame.

38 Roe Skidmore, 1.000, 0 HR, 0 RBI

Roe Skidmore's September 17, 1970 appearance for the Cubs was his only major-league game. He played minor-league ball through 1977. For thirty-two years, he was an insurance agent with AXA Advisors, achieving the AXA Equitable Hall of Fame. He also has worked for New Horizons Insurance Marketing and has scouted for several major-league teams.

25 Willie Smith, .216, 5 HR, 24 RBI

Willie Smith's last major-league season was 1971 with the Cincinnati Reds. He played for the Nankai Hawks in Japan in 1972 and 1973. An excellent singer, his vocals were recorded for the *Cub Power* record of 1969. After retirement, Smith worked in construction and at several jobs for the city of Oxford, Alabama. He also coached for a semipro team, the Hobson City Tigers, and at Jacksonville State University in Alabama. He died on January 16, 2006, at age sixty-six.

OUTFIELDERS

6 John Callison, .264, 19 HR, 68 RBI

John Callison's last year in the major leagues was 1973 with the New York Yankees. In retirement, he worked as a car salesman and a bartender and was a popular fixture at the Phillies' fantasy camps. He died on October 12, 2006, at age sixty-seven.

29 Brock Davis, .000, 0 HR, 0 RBI

Brock Davis became the Cubs' regular center fielder in 1971 and finished his major-league career with the Milwaukee Brewers in 1972.

29 Tommy Davis, .262, 2 HR, 8 RBI

Tommy Davis was one of the top designated hitters from 1973 to 1975 with the Baltimore Orioles, and his last season was 1976 with the Kansas City Royals. After retirement, he worked for the Los Angeles Dodgers as a minor-league instructor and in community relations and as a coach for the Seattle Mariners.

20 Boots Day, .250, 0 HR, 0 RBI

Boots Day's last season was 1974 with the Montreal Expos. After retirement, he served as a hitting coach with the Evansville Otters and Normal CornBelters of the Frontier League and the Calgary Vipers of the Golden Baseball League.

23 Jimmie Hall, .094, 0 HR, 1 RBI

A star with the Minnesota Twins in the early 1960s, Jimmie Hall finished his career in 1970 with the Atlanta Braves. After retirement, he worked as a woodworker and for a trucking company in Wilson, North Carolina.

28 Jim Hickman, .315, 32 HR, 115 RBI

Another Cub regular traded in the 1973 postseason purge, Jim Hickman finished his major-league career with the St. Louis Cardinals in 1974. He returned to his native Tennessee to farm after his retirement and was inducted into the Tennessee Sports Hall of Fame in 1996. He also worked as a minor-league hitting instructor for the Cincinnati Reds. "Gentleman Jim" died on June 25, 2016, at age seventy-nine.

24 Cleo James, .210, 3 HR, 14 RBI

Cleo James was a baseball and football star at Riverside, California Junior College. He decided on baseball and was a member of the Pacific Coast League All-Star team in 1969 and finished third in the league in batting average. James remained with the Cubs through his last major-league season, 1973. My wife, Anne Nordhaus-Bike, considers James her favorite 1970 Cub.

8 Joe Pepitone, .268, 12 HR, 44 RBI

Joe Pepitone during his playing career in Chicago operated a wig and hairdressing salon, One Touch of Glamor, and a bar, Joe Pepitone's Thing. He had his best year in the major leagues with the Cubs in 1971. Pepitone ended his major-league career with the Atlanta Braves in 1973. He later played baseball in Japan. As a minor-league coach for the New York Yankees, he taught Don Mattingly how to play first base; Pepitone later coached for the Yankees at the major-league level as well. He has been sober since 2000.

20 Al Spangler, .143, 1 HR, 1 RBI

Al Spangler's last season was 1971 with the Cubs. He served as a coach with the Cubs through 1974. After retirement, he became an algebra teacher, baseball coach and athletic director at Hargrave High School in Huffman, Texas, where he coached future major-league pitcher Keith Foulke.

26 Billy Williams, .322, 42 HR, 129 RBI

Billy Williams, known for his perfect "sweet" swing, remained with the Cubs through 1974, and then they dealt him to the Oakland Athletics, where he finally saw postseason play. He retired after the 1976 season. Williams spent nineteen years coaching in the major leagues with the Cubs, Athletics and Cleveland Indians. The National Baseball Hall of Fame inducted him in 1987. The Cubs honored him by placing a statue of him outside Wrigley Field in 2010.

MANAGER

2 Leo Durocher

The Cubs fired Leo Durocher in the middle of the 1972 season, and he finished the year managing the Houston Astros. He also managed the Astros in 1973. Durocher played an important role in the integration of Major League Baseball in the 1940s. He enjoyed associating with movie stars and entertainers. The phrase "Nice guys finish last" is attributed to Durocher. He died on October 7, 1991, at age eighty-six. The National Baseball Hall of Fame inducted him in 1994.

COACHES

5 Joey Amalfitano

Joey Amalfitano later served as a coach for the San Francisco Giants, San Diego Padres, Los Angeles Dodgers and Cincinnati Reds; as a consultant for baseball operations with the Dodgers; and as special assistant for player development for the Giants. He managed the Cubs in parts of 1979 and 1980 and all of 1981.

3 Joe Becker

Joe Becker was a former catcher who became a pitching coach. He retired from coaching during the 1970 season because of heart trouble but lived for many years after. Becker died on January 11, 1998, at age eighty-nine.

37 Herman Franks

Herman Franks was another former catcher who became a pitching coach. He managed the Cubs in 1978, 1979 and part of the season in 1980. Franks served as the Cubs interim general manager in 1981. An astute businessperson, he also worked as a financial advisor. Franks died on March 30, 2009, at age ninety-five.

7 Harry "Peanuts" Lowrey

Peanuts Lowrey was a Cub coach through 1971 and came back to coach the team again from 1977 to 1981. He also was a coach for the California Angels in 1972. Lowrey had appeared as a baseball player in the 1952 Ronald Reagan movie biography of Grover Cleveland Alexander, *The Winning Team*. He died on July 2, 1996, at age sixty-eight.

4 Verlon "Rube" Walker

Verlon Walker and his brother Albert, another ballplayer and coach, both went by the nickname "Rube." Verlon Walker had been one of the Cubs' College of Coaches, whose members took turns managing the team, in the early 1960s. Durocher planned to make him the Cubs' pitching coach for 1971, but he died of leukemia on March 24 of that year at age forty-two. The Cubs established the Rube Walker Blood Center at Northwestern Memorial Hospital in his honor.

BROADCASTERS

Jack Brickhouse, WGN-TV

Jack Brickhouse served as the play-by-play announcer for the Cubs on WGN-TV from 1948 to 1981, known for his signature shout of "Hey, hey" when a Cub player hit a home run. He received the Ford C. Frick Award from the National Baseball Hall of Fame in 1983 and was inducted into the American Sportscasters Association Hall of Fame in 1985. In his career, he also was the broadcaster for the New York Giants, Chicago White Sox, Chicago Bears and Chicago Bulls. He died on August 6, 1988, at age eighty-two.

Lloyd Pettit, WGN-TV

Lloyd Pettit's last year broadcasting the Cubs' games on WGN-TV was 1970. Broadcasting hockey was his first love, and he moved to WMAQ Radio when the Blackhawks did later that year. "Shot and a goal!" was his trademark phrase. He later owned the Milwaukee Admirals minor-league hockey team and was a part owner of the Milwaukee Bucks of the National Basketball Association. He died on November 11, 2003, at age seventy-six.

Lou Boudreau, WGN Radio

After a Hall of Fame baseball career and managing the Cleveland Indians and Boston Red Sox, Lou Boudreau broadcast Cub games on WGN Radio and TV from 1957 to 1987, with the exception of 1960, when he managed the team. His mangling of players' names gave listeners a chuckle, but his insider's knowledge of the game was unparalleled. He died on August 10, 2001, at age eighty-four.

Vince Lloyd, WGN Radio

Vince Lloyd broadcast Cub games on WGN Radio and TV for more than thirty years. Songwriters included his signature phrase "Holy mackerel" in the Cubs' fight song. When broadcasting a Chicago White Sox game, he became the first baseball announcer to interview a sitting president when he spoke with John F. Kennedy. He also broadcast Chicago Bears, Chicago Fire and college football games. He died on July 3, 2003 at age eighty-six.

THE '69ERS

Oscar Gamble, .262, 1 HR, 19 RBI for Philadelphia in 1970

Oscar Gamble played his last major-league season for the Chicago White Sox in 1985. Gamble had the biggest Afro hairstyle in the major leagues in the 1970s. He played in four American League Championship Series and two World Series with the New York Yankees and was the best player on the 1977 South Side Hit Men White Sox. In retirement, Gamble worked as a player agent and discotheque owner. He died on January 31, 2018 at age sixty-eight.

Ken Johnson, 0-0, 7.50 ERA for Montreal in 1970

Ken Johnson finished his major-league career with the Montreal Expos in 1970. He pitched a no-hitter, a 1–0 loss, for the Houston Colt .45s in 1964. In retirement, Johnson worked for Palm Beach Atlantic College in West Palm Beach, Florida, supervising the work-study program, and he coached baseball at Louisiana College in Pineville and Louisiana Baptist University in Shreveport. He died on November 21, 2015 at age eighty-two.

Jim Qualls, .111, 0 HR, 1 RBI for Montreal in 1970

Jim Qualls's last year in the majors was with the Chicago White Sox in 1972. He played for the Kintetsu Buffaloes in Japan in 1972 and 1973. He has worked as a welder and a farmer, raised livestock and worked in the livestock feed business.

Dick Selma, 8-9, 2.75 ERA, 22 saves for Philadelphia in 1970

Dick Selma last pitched in the majors for the Milwaukee Brewers in 1974. After the Cubs traded him to Philadelphia, he refused the Phillies' management's request for him to cheerlead as he had in Chicago. In retirement, he worked in food processing, served as an assistant coach at Fresno City College in Fresno, California, and worked as the pitching coach at Clovis High School in Clovis, California. He died on August 29, 2001, at age fifty-seven.

Don Young, Minor Leagues in 1970

A former Texas League All-Star, Don Young had his last major-league season with the Cubs in 1969. He played minor-league ball through 1972 and then retired. He has worked as a machinist, groundskeeper and truck driver.

Owner

Philip K. Wrigley

Philip Wrigley took over the Wm. Wrigley Jr. gum company and the Chicago Cubs on the death of his father in 1932. Planning to add lights to Wrigley Field for the 1942 season, he instead donated the steel to the U.S. Navy when World War II began, and Wrigley Field had no lights for the rest of his life. Philip Wrigley maximized media coverage by broadcasting as many games on radio and TV as possible, and he coined the phrase "Beautiful Wrigley Field." He hired Leo Durocher to turn the also-ran Cubs into a contender. Wrigley died on April 12, 1977, at age eighty-two.

Vice-President and General Manager

John Holland

John Holland served as vice-president and general manager of the Cubs from 1956 to 1975. He built the contending Cubs of the 1960s and 1970s by signing or trading for stars Glenn Beckert, Randy Hundley, Ferguson Jenkins, Don Kessinger, Ron Santo and Billy Williams, but he also engineered or allowed the disastrous trades of Lou Brock, Oscar Gamble, Dick Selma and Ted Abernathy. Holland died on July 15, 1979, at age sixty-nine.

Beautiful Wrigley Field

In 1970, from home plate, the distance down the left-field line was 355 feet; down the right-field line was 353 feet; and to straight-away center, 400 feet. The height of the outfield wall was 11.5 feet, made slightly higher with the addition of the concrete triangles at the top of the wall after the first home stand.

Wrigley Field had 3,254 reserved seats in the first tier (first ten rows); 6,363 in the second tier (next twelve rows); and 4,618 in the upper deck; these were commonly known as "box" seats. There were 19,182 seats in the lower- and upper-deck grandstands and 3,250 in the bleachers. The total was 36,667, and prices ranged from $1.00 for bleachers, to $1.75 for the grandstand, to $3.50 for first-tier box seats. The park still sold children's tickets to the grandstand for $1.00. Friday was Ladies' Day, when girls and women age fourteen and older were admitted free.

Weekday games started at 1:30 p.m.; Saturday and Sunday games started at 1:15 p.m.; and doubleheaders started at 12:30 p.m. When umpires called for play to cease because of darkness, as Wrigley Field had no lights, the game was suspended for later resumption.

The Cubs' scorecard urged fans to "lunch well—and economically. You'll enjoy a snack at Wrigley Field, where we serve only the best of food and drinks, and at prices lower than you'll pay elsewhere." Prices for food and other products were as follows:

$0.05—chewing gum, Wrigley's of course

$0.10—pencil

$0.15—small bag of peanuts, popcorn, frostick (like a frosty malt, only on a stick), small Coca-Cola or Fresca, coffee, cheap cigar, scorecard

$0.20—milk, medium cigar

$0.25—large bag of peanuts, French fries, frosty malt, taffy apple, large Coca-Cola or Fresca, lemonade, orangeade

$0.30—expensive cigar

$0.35—hot dog, ham sandwich, picture package of Cubs' players

$0.40—smokie link, sold only from cooking carts parked on the concourse between the box seats and grandstand in the lower deck; cheese pizza

$0.45—bratwurst, barbecued beef sandwich

$0.50—hamburger, sausage pizza, Old Style beer, Schlitz beer, cigarettes, roster book, lapel badge

$0.60—corned beef sandwich

$0.75—pennant (if only it had been so easy for the Cubs to get one!)

$1.00—baseball bat pen-and-pencil set

$1.25—ten miniature National League pennants (two years into expansion, they still did not have pennants for the Montreal Expos and San Diego Padres), bobble head doll, cheap cap

$1.50—T-shirt, bat rack bank

$2.00—batting helmet (had a label that said not to use when playing baseball, but of course we did)

$2.50—expensive cap, kids' sweatshirt

$3.00—autographed baseball (the holder cost an extra $1.25); adult sweatshirt

$9.00—kid's jacket

$11.00—adult jacket

Only rarely did a parent spring for any of the items that were more than $1.

Vendors who walked around the park and sold hot dogs, pop, peanuts and beer did well. Those who sold the other items, not so much. Beer was in glass bottles, but vendors would pour it into a cup before providing it to the customer. No matter what they sold, vendors seldom made it to the upper deck, so if you sat up there, you pretty much had to go to the concession stands.

The press box and broadcast booth were under the upper deck then, not in it.

The modest bleacher entrance at the corner of Waveland and Sheffield Avenues, where a ticket could be procured for one dollar. *Chicago History Museum, ICHi-024309; F.S. Dauwalter, photographer.*

The small Cub dugout was on the third-base side, and the equally small visitors' dugout was on the first-base side. The players' clubhouses were among the smallest in baseball, and fans could watch the visitors' players enter and exit their clubhouse through a staircase protected by a chain-link fence below the lower deck.

Twelve pennants, one for each National League team, flew from the yardarms above the center-field scoreboard in the order of the standing of each division on the morning of the game. Like today, after the game, the Cubs put up the "W" flag for a win and the "L" flag after a loss. The scoreboard, as today, measured twenty-seven feet high and seventy-five feet wide.

"Wrigley was just a great ballpark, when seats were still cheap, not a shrine where families hand out hundreds of dollars for four tickets," Kipp said.[117]

Minor Leagues

The Cubs' affiliates in the minor leagues were the Tacoma Cubs in Washington State in the Pacific Coast League (AAA), the San Antonio Missions in the Texas League (AA), the Quincy Cubs in Illinois in the Midwest League (A), the Huron Cubs in South Dakota in the Northern League (A) and the Caldwell Cubs in Idaho in the Pioneer League (Rookie).

NOTES

Preface

1. Interview with Karl Matuszewski, April 18, 2020.

Chapter 1

2. "Cubs, Fans Say Thanks," *Chicago Sun-Times*.

Chapter 2

3. Sullivan, "All-Star 2nd Baseman."
4. *1970 Chicago Cubs Official Roster Book, Mid-Season Edition*, 3.
5. Munzel, "Cubs Send Gamble, Selma to Phillies."
6. *1969 Chicago Cubs Official Roster Book, Mid-Season Edition*, 5.
7. Feldmann, *Miracle Collapse*, 57.

Chapter 3

8. Treder, "Williams-Santo Cubs: 1970–1973."
9. Freedman, *Ernie Banks*, 93.

10. Italie, "Cardinals Hall of Famer."
11. Nathanson, *People's History of Baseball*, 104.
12. Ibid.
13. Talley, *Cubs of '69*, 236.
14. Munzel, "Cubs Send Gamble, Selma to Phillies."
15. Ibid.
16. Talley, *Cubs of '69*, 237.
17. Holtzman, "Cubs Get Boots Day for Nye."

Chapter 4

18. Munzel, "Rookie Hurlers Give Cubs Lift."
19. Vaccaro, "Origins of the Pitching Rotation."
20. Talley, *Cubs of '69*, 253.
21. Vaccaro, "Origins of the Pitching Rotation."
22. Munzel, "Leo to Switch Banks, Callison."
23. Fowler, "Decker's Sparkling Pitching Gives Cal Chance," *Sporting News*.
24. Leo Durocher, "Cubs Deeper in Reserves," *Chicago Sun-Times*, April 5, 1970.
25. Munzel, "Cubs Get Met Martin for Bobb."
26. Ibid.

Chapter 5

27. Munzel, "Cubs Won't Collapse."
28. Talley, "No Cub Slump."
29. Packard, *Discovering Your Devine Destiny*, 15.
30. *1970 Chicago Cubs Official Roster Book, Mid-Season Edition*, 42.
31. Interview with Ken Hennig, April 22, 2020.
32. "Hundley Knee in Cast," *Chicago Sun-Times*.
33. Corbett, "Steve Barber."
34. "Cubs Romp to 9th in Row," *Chicago Sun-Times*.
35. Claerbaut, *Durocher's Cubs*, 138.
36. Langford, *Game Is Never Over*, 149.

Chapter 6

37. Munzel, "Cubs Lose All Decisions."
38. WGN-TV broadcast, May 12, 1970.
39. Goddard, "Fan 'Boots' Ernie's Blast."
40. Griffin, "Ernie, the Eternal Boy, Exults."
41. Holtzman, "Cub Homers Bump Sox."
42. Ibid.
43. Langford, *Game Is Never Over*, 150.
44. Claerbaut, *Durocher's Cubs*, 164.
45. *Kansas City Royals Yearbook*.

Chapter 7

46. "Military Call-Ups May Decide," *New York Times*.
47. Claerbaut, *Durocher's Cubs*, 135.
48. Langford, *Game Is Never Over*, 156.
49. Claerbaut, *Durocher's Cubs*, 140.
50. Goddard, "Fan 'Boots' Ernie's Blast."
51. "1969 Replay?," *Chicago Sun-Times*.
52. Corbett, "Milt Pappas."
53. Bouton, *Ball Four*, 348.
54. Sullivan, "All-Star 2nd Baseman."
55. Goddard, "Former Cubs Miss Bums."
56. Ramos, "Hank Aguirre."
57. Talley, *Cubs of '69*, 257.
58. Claerbaut, *Durocher's Cubs*, 139.

Chapter 8

59. "Cub Pitching Torn to Pieces," *Chicago Sun-Times*.
60. Santo, *For Love of Ivy*, 107.
61. Talley, *Cubs of '69*, 247.
62. Costello, "Juan Pizarro."
63. "Cubs on Upbeat," *Chicago Sun-Times*.
64. "Banks on Disabled List," *Chicago Sun-Times*.
65. MacLennan, "Chicago Cubs History."

66. Pepitone, *Joe, You Coulda Made Us Proud*.
67. Ibid., 220.
68. "'Hair' at Wrigley," *Chicago Sun-Times*.
69. *Chicago Sun-Times*, August 2, 1970.
70. Goddard, "Former Cubs Miss Bums."
71. "Charging Cubs Drop Reds Twice," *Chicago Sun-Times*.

Chapter 9

72. Claerbaut, *Durocher's Cubs*, 146.
73. Ibid., 149.
74. Pepitone, *Joe, You Coulda Made Us Proud*, 228.
75. Berg, "Joe Pepitone Says."
76. Munzel, "Trading Abby."
77. *Chicago Sun-Times*, August 17, 1970.
78. Pepitone, *Joe, You Coulda Made Us Proud*, 228.
79. Dunn, "Joe Decker."
80. Hochman, "Survivors of '64: Johnny Callison," 175.
81. Callison, with Sletten, *Johnny Callison Story*, 182.
82. "Cub Victory, Weird, Wonderful," *Chicago Today*.
83. Langford, *Game Is Never Over*, 153.
84. "Cubs Leap into 2d" and "Cubs Game Out!"

Chapter 10

85. Holtzman, "Cubs Take 3–2 Gift."
86. Ibid.
87. Gleason, "'Game's Never Over.'"
88. Holtzman, "Win with Wind Is Cubs Motto."
89. Stewart and Hirsch, "Tommy Davis."
90. Ibid.
91. Holtzman, "Cubs Nip Phils 5–3."
92. Santo, *For Love of Ivy*, 103.
93. Holtzman, "Cubs Slow, Cautious, Uninspired."

Chapter 11

94. Silver, "Vorping Their Way Into the Pantheon."
95. Langford, *Game Is Never Over*, 154.
96. Treder, "Williams-Santo Cubs: 1970–1973."
97. Holtzman, "'Don't Bust Up Cubs.'"
98. Holtzman, "Cubs Slow, Cautious, Uninspired."
99. Langford, *Game Is Never Over*, 156.
100. Timms, "Confident Terry Hughes."
101. Costello, "Roe Skidmore."
102. Holtzman, "Kauffman to Revive the Royals' Academy," 25.
103. Claerbaut, *Durocher's Cubs*.
104. "Hundley the Answer?" *Sporting News*.
105. Slowinski, "Pythagorean Win-Loss."
106. "1970 Chicago Cubs."
107. "1970 Cincinnati Reds."
108. Talley, "No Cub Slump."
109. Mitchell, "It's Like Old Times."
110. Talley, *Cubs of '69*, 56.

Chapter 13

111. Talley, *Cubs of '69*, 120.
112. Interview with Al Kipp, April 18, 2020.
113. Feldmann, *Miracle Collapse*, 251.

Chapter 14

114. Bike, "Best Interest of Baseball," 50.
115. Feldmann, *Miracle Collapse*, 57.
116. Bike, "Best Interest of Baseball."

Chapter 16

117. Interview with Al Kipp, April 18, 2020.

BIBLIOGRAPHY

Books

Callison, John, with Sletten, John Austin. *The Johnny Callison Story*. New York: Vantage Press, 1991.

Claerbaut, David. *Durocher's Cubs*. Dallas: Taylor Publishing, 2000.

Feldmann, Doug. *Miracle Collapse: The 1969 Chicago Cubs*. Lincoln: University of Nebraska Press, 2009.

Freedman, Lew. *Ernie Banks: The Life and Career of "Mr. Cub."* Jefferson, NC: McFarland, 2019.

Hochman, Stan. "The Survivors of '64: Johnny Callison." In *The Phillies Reader*, by Richard Orodenker. Philadelphia: Temple University Press, 1996.

Kansas City Royals Yearbook. Kansas City, MO: Kansas City Royals, 1971.

Langford, Jim. *The Game Is Never Over: An Appreciative History of the Chicago Cubs*. South Bend, IN: Icarus Press, 1982.

Nathanson, Mitchell. *A People's History of Baseball*. Champaign: University of Illinois Press, 2015.

1970 Chicago Cubs Official Roster Book, Mid-Season Edition. Chicago: Chicago National League Ball Club Inc., 1970.

1969 Chicago Cubs Official Roster Book, Mid-Season Edition. Chicago: Chicago National League Ball Club Inc., 1969.

Packard, Bill. *Discovering your Devine Destiny: Out of the Salt Mine*. Camarillo, CA: Xulon Press, 2007.

Pepitone, Joe. *Joe, You Coulda Made Us Proud*. New York: Dell Publishing, 1975.

Santo, Ron. *For Love of Ivy*. Chicago: Bonus Books, 1993.
Talley, Rick. *The Cubs of '69*. Chicago: Contemporary Books, 1989.

Interviews

Hennig, Ken. Interview with author. April 22, 2020.
Kipp, Al. Interview with author. April 18, 2020.
Matuszewski, Karl. Interview with author. April 18, 2020.

Journals, Magazines and Newspapers

Berg, Ted. "Joe Pepitone Says He Used to Hide His Drugs in Wrigley Field's Ivy." *USA Today*, July 17, 2015.
Bike, William S. "The Best Interest of Baseball." *Delta Epsilon Sigma Journal* no. 2 (1992).
Chicago Sun-Times. August 2, 1970.
———. August 17, 1970.
———. "Banks on Disabled List; End of Line?" July 23, 1970.
———. "Charging Cubs Drop Reds Twice." August 1, 1970, 70.
———. "Cub Pitching Torn to Pieces 16–14." July 4, 1970.
———. "Cubs, Fans Say Thanks." October 3, 1969.
———. "Cubs Leap into 2d; A Game out of 1st," and "Cubs Game Out! Pepitone Homer Rips Padres 3–0." August 31, 1970.
———. "Cubs on Upbeat, March Past Phils." July 13, 1970.
———. "Cubs Romp to 9th in Row." April 26, 1970.
———. "'Hair' at Wrigley: Pepitone a Cub." July 30, 1970.
———. "Hundley Knee in Cast; No Surgery." April 23, 1970.
———. "1969 Replay? Help, Help! Cubs No. 2 After Met 9–5, 6–1 Sweep." June 25, 1970.
Chicago Today. "Cub Victory, Weird, Wonderful." August 28, 1970.
Fowler, Bob. "Decker's Sparkling Pitching Gives Cal Chance to Chuckle." *Sporting News*, May 11, 1974.
Gleason, Bill. "'Game's Never Over,' Cubs Prove." *Chicago Sun-Times*, September 14, 1970.
Goddard, Joe. "Fan 'Boots' Ernie's Blast." *Chicago Sun-Times*, May 13, 1970.
———. "Former Cubs Miss Bums, Ray's Bleachers, *Chicago Sun-Times*, August 12, 1970.

Griffin, Jack. "Ernie, the Eternal Boy, Exults: Homer No. 500!" *Chicago Sun-Times*, May 13, 1970.

Holtzman, Jerome. "Cub Homers Bump Sox in Benefit." *Chicago Sun-Times*, May 22, 1970.

———. "Cubs Get Boots Day for Nye." *Chicago Sun-Times*, December 5, 1969.

———. "Cubs Slow, Cautious, Uninspired." *Chicago Sun-Times*.

———. "Cubs Take 3–2 Gift from Pirates." *Chicago Sun-Times*, September 14, 1970.

———. "Cubs Nip Phils 5–3." *Chicago Sun-Times*, September 28, 1970.

———. "'Don't Bust Up Cubs,' Beckert Asks Bosses." *Sporting News*, October 31, 1970.

———. "Kauffman to Revive the Royals' Academy." *Sporting News*. July 1, 1978.

———. "Win with Wind Is Cubs Motto; Still a Game Out." *Chicago Sun-Times*. September 16, 1970.

"Hundley The Answer?" *Sporting News*, September 4, 1971.

Italie, Hillel. "Cardinals Hall of Famer." *Chicago Sun-Times*, September 7, 2020.

Mitchell, Fred. "It's Like Old Times to Santo," *Chicago Tribune*, February 17, 1986.

Munzel, Edgar. "Cubs Get Met Martin for Bobb." *Chicago Sun-Times*, March 30, 1970.

———. "Cubs Lose All Decisions." *Chicago Sun-Times*, May 3, 1970, 138.

———. "Cubs Send Gamble, Selma to Phillies for Callison." *Chicago Sun-Times*, November 19, 1969.

———. "Cubs Won't Collapse." *Chicago Sun-Times*, April 5, 1970.

———. "Leo to Switch Banks, Callison." *Chicago Sun-Times*, March 6, 1970.

———. "Rookie Hurlers Give Cubs Lift." *Chicago Sun-Times*, March 8, 1970.

———. "Trading Abby Was Cubs' Big Goof." *Chicago Sun-Times*, August 17, 1970.

New York Times. "Military Call-Ups May Decide Major League Pennant Races." June 7, 1970.

Ramos, George. "Hank Aguirre: An Even Bigger Hero Off the Diamond." *Los Angeles Times*, September 26, 1994.

Silver, Nate. "Vorping Their Way Into the Pantheon." *New York Times Magazine*, April 3, 2011.

Sullivan, Paul. "All-Star 2nd Baseman 'The Glue' for '69 Cubs." *Chicago Tribune*. April 13, 2020.

———. "Milt Pappas Always Will Be Remembered for the One Call That Went Against Him." *Chicago Tribune*, April 20, 2016.

Talley, Rick. "No Cub Slump in 'Year of Power.'" *Chicago Today*, April 5, 1970.

Timms, Leslie. "Confident Terry Hughes." *Spartanburg (SC) Herald-Journal*, February 21, 1971.

Vaccaro, Frank. "Origins of the Pitching Rotation." *Baseball Research Journal* (Fall 2011).

Online

Corbett, Warren. "Milt Pappas." Society for American Baseball Research. www.sabr.org/bioproj/person/44e56ef0.

———. "Steve Barber." Society for American Baseball Research. www.sabr.org/bioproj/person/2e4cfa6c.

Costello, Rory. "Juan Pizarro." Society for American Baseball Research. www.sabr.org/bioproj/person/bb767482.

———. "Roe Skidmore." Society for American Baseball Research. www.sabr.org/bioproj/person/ab0aaf2e.

Dunn, Steve. "Joe Decker." Society for American Baseball Research. www.sabr.org/bioproj/person/3ddbb871.

MacLennan, Ashley. "Chicago Cubs History: Joe Pepitone and the 1970 Cubs." *Bleed Cubbie Blue*, December 29, 2019. www.bleedcubbieblue.com.

"1970 Chicago Cubs Statistics." Baseball Reference. www.baseball-reference.com/teams/CHC/1970.shtml.

"1970 Cincinnati Reds." Baseball Reference. www.baseball-reference.com/teams/CIN/1970.shtml.

Sharp, Andrew. "Willie Smith." Society for American Baseball Research. www.sabr.org/bioproj/person/f741d5af.

Slowinski, Steve. "Pythagorean Win-Loss." FanGraphs, February 26, 2010. www.library.fangraphs.com/principles/expected-wins-and-losses.

Sternman, Mark. "Glenn Beckert." Society for American Baseball Research. www.sabr.org/bioproj/person/97ff644b.

Stewart, Mark, and Paul Hirsch. "Tommy Davis." Society for American Baseball Research. www.sabr.org/bioproj/person/664f669f.

Treder, Steve. "The Williams-Santo Cubs: 1970–1973." *Hardball Times*, February 22, 2005. www.hardballtimes.com.

WhatIfSports.com. www.whatifsports.com.

Television

WGN-TV broadcast, May 12, 1970.

INDEX

ABOUT THE AUTHOR

William S. Bike wrote the books *Streets of the Near West Side, Winning Political Campaigns* and *Celebrating a Proud Past* and edited the book *Essays on Earl Renfroe: A Man of Firsts.* Associate editor of the newspaper *Gazette Chicago*, he also works as a freelance writer. Formerly, he directed communications for Loyola University Chicago, the University of Chicago Graduate School of Business and the University of Illinois Chicago College of Dentistry. Bike has earned more than fifty awards in journalism, publications, media relations and alumni relations, including three Peter Lisagor Awards, the top honors in Chicago journalism.

He and his wife, Anne Nordhaus-Bike, live in Chicago. He attended his first Chicago Cubs game on August 29, 1967, when his mother and another mom brought the kids to the game on Ladies' Day.

For more information, log on to www.centralparkcommunications.com or, email billbike@anbcommunications.com.

Visit us at
www.historypress.com
....